WAR WAS CRUEL

Love & Peace

1

IN THE VIETNAM WAR | 1966-1969

MYEONG-SEOK JEONG

Queries:
Evergreen Publishing Corporation
Email | vtbooktranslate@gmail.com
Address | 11428 187th St. Artesia,Ca 90701 USA

First published in Korean in S. Korea in 2018 by Myeong Moon

전쟁은 잔인했다
사랑과 평화다

베트남전쟁 참전기, 1966-1969
저자: 정명석

Author: Myeong-Seok Jeong
English Translation: Jennifer Kwon, Princess Joo, Naomi Kim, Jennifer Park, Hana Kim
Graphics and Layout Designer: Sharon Robinson
English Editor: Esther Maher
Chief Editor and Project Manager: Jennifer Kwon

The majority of the graphics and drawings were taken from the original book published in Korean. Additional graphics were added to the English copy.

Author: Myeong-Seok Jeong

MEET THE AUTHOR

The author of the book was born in 1945 in Wolmyeongdong, Geumsan-gun, South Chungcheong Province, South Korea. He prayed in the mountains for 21 years starting in his teens and completed two tours of the Vietnam War while always holding firm to his faith. For more than 50 years, he preached the Word he learned from Jesus to people from 70 nations, and has written many books. In 1995, he was acknowledged nationally as a poet through the monthly Literary Society and published five best-selling volumes of poetry. He is also active as an artist. He has held 13 individual exhibitions and was selected as a best artist at the 2011 Argentine Art Fair, which was recognized both in Korea and abroad.

Chapter 3: The Day I Guarded the Frontlines

Chapter 4: A Miraculous Close Call During Helicopter Training

Chapter 7: It Was No Joke

Chapter 8 : Love Him!

Note This book is based on true stories, but some of the names in this book are aliases or abbreviated, while others are real.

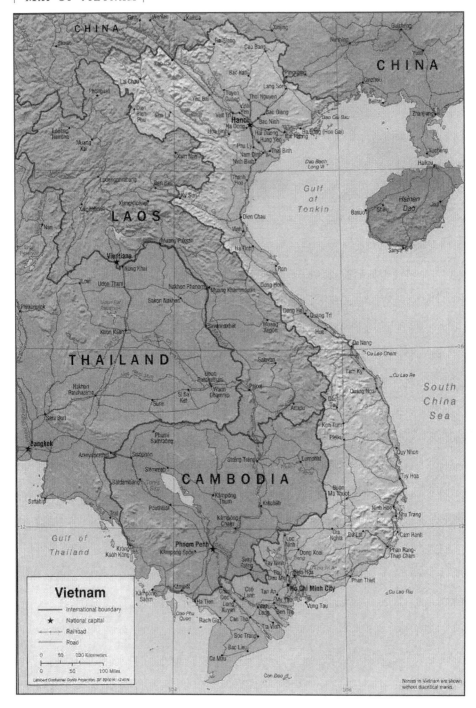

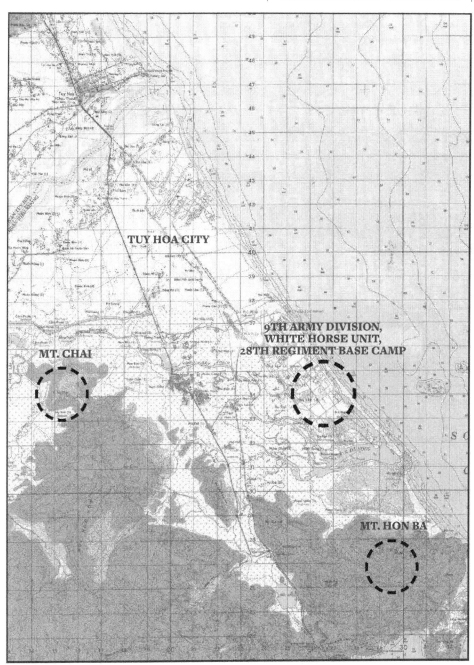

TUY HOA CITY

9TH ARMY DIVISION,
WHITE HORSE UNIT,
28TH REGIMENT BASE CAMP

MT. CHAI

MT. HON BA

From the White Horse Unit base camp situated near the
Tuy Hoa city, on the left was Honba Mountain, and on the
right was Chai Mountain with the sea at our back.

A Confession of Faith Before God, a Written Record of the Fulfillment of God's Will

COMMANDER-IN-CHIEF OF THE KOREAN ARMED FORCES IN VIETNAM | *Myeong-Shin Chae*

This book is the record of one young soldier who fought fiercely for his country and his people on a battlefield of blood, even at the crossroad between life and death.

About 40 years ago, at the same time and under the same sky, we fought together as comrades in the Vietnam War. I find it deeply moving that one of the soldiers who was under my guidance is now able to publish his experiences in a book. He carried out his mission with distinction, and as a fellow comrade, I congratulate him.

This book realistically portrays life on the battlefield and expresses the author's bitter struggle to act with love and peace in that jungle, that chaotic war zone of fear and doubt.

This is the author's personal confession of faith before God, and at the same time, it is the written record of the fulfillment of God's will. All wars are sin and wickedness created by man, but this war reveals a deeper story, for it sheds new light on the hidden, higher level providence of God.

In my memoirs of the Vietnam War, I also confessed that I had lived under God's protection. Yet as a veteran and a fellow traveler on the path of life, I felt particularly touched by the writings of President Jeong. Truly, he depicts the experience of witnessing God's salvation in a most moving way.

To President Jeong, who has realized the will of this history, who prays for peace for all mankind, and who, even today, leads countless young people on the true path, I would like to express my sincere gratitude. May God bless you forever.

March, 2007

Myeong-Shin Chae.

The Confession of One Devoted Warrior
Who Truly Cherished Life

Battalion Commander to the Korean armed forces in Vietnam (Colonel of the Reserve Forces) | *Yeong-Woo Lee*

In the Vietnam War, I served as the commander of 1st Battalion, 28th Regiment, 9th Division, ROKA (Republic of Korea Army), the White Horse Division.

I still remember that day 50 years ago, standing in front of the Capitol Building in Seoul as the nation farewelled its troops leaving for Vietnam. The president at that time hung a lei of flowers around my neck and told me to come back victorious.

The man in the picture above is Lt. Col. Stanchkam, commander of the U.S. Air Force, with whom we worked to block the Vietcong attacks. Those memories are still so vivid. I remember pouring sand into sandbags provided by Stanchkam and loading them onto vehicles for troop protection. This helped us relocate safely to the area where the operation was to take place and then carry out the operation successfully without losing even one soldier.

My proudest accomplishment of the Vietnam War was leading the 1st Battalion, and among all the companies in that battalion, I am especially proud of the elite 3rd Company, led by Commander Chan-Ki Min (General, Reserve Forces) that was labeled the Quick Reaction Force (QRF) which is similar to SWAT. They carried out more operations and fought more battles than any other unit, yet incurred the least number of casualties.

Min was my most trusted commander at the time, so I didn't think much about 3rd Company's brilliant performance. However, through this book, I came to know some of the astonishing stories behind that success.

Going into the Vietnam War, Jeong had just one desperate wish. Unlike those around him, he didn't hope to use his war money to buy television sets and cassette recorders. Instead, he earnestly hoped that all his fellow soldiers would return home alive.

"War belongs to God, and your life is something you cannot exchange or regain, even for all the riches in the world." Jeong always kept these words in his heart, and this book tells the story of how much he cherished life while living and fighting in Vietnam.

I worked closely with General Myeong-Shin Chae, Commander-in-chief of the Republic of Korea Army in Vietnam, and he, too, put the lives of his men first in everything he did. He agreed to take the position of Commander-in-Chief only under the condition that the Korean forces were permitted to operate independently. His mindset clearly demonstrated the love he had for his men.

General Chae knew that if South Korean forces were under the control of the U.S. military, Koreans would be deployed to the fiercest battlefields, and thus his men would suffer greater casualties.

'No battle in Vietnam is worth winning at the risk of your comrades' lives.' That was Commander Chae's philosophy, and it went hand in hand with Jeong's life, which was based on loving people and valuing their lives. They were connected like a tree and its fruit.

Jeong was a key player in the Vietnam War. It's safe to say that he was the soldier that best understood and followed the directions of Chae, one of the greatest military commanders. I remember he said, "True victory is not achieved by killing the enemy." I can still picture him saying this confidently and fiercely. He would say it on the battlefield, even to his direct superiors.

Jeong was sent to Vietnam twice and fought for a total of 25 months. During that time, there was only one casualty from 3rd Company, but during the six months between his first and second tour when he was not in Vietnam, 3rd Company incurred over 24 casualties. This book accurately relays these facts. Truly, Jeong's love and respect for human life transformed the battlefield.

Before entering the battlefield, Jeong would find out how to prepare and what to watch out for in that day's battle through dreams and inspiration, and that knowledge saved the lives of many of his fellow soldiers. This book shares those amazing stories, and I attest to the truth of the stories as someone who experienced similar things while fighting in the Korean War.

One of the fiercest battles I fought was the Battle of Gachilbong, a place also known as the Highlands of Kim Il-Sung. Before this particular battle, my mother came to me in a dream and said, "Your troops are surrounded." The prophetic nature of the dream made me and my troops even more alert that day, and it was this mental clarity and preparedness that allowed us to defeat the enemy. They attempted to entrap us, but we were prepared and left the battlefield with our lives.

This book also tells the story of Operation Hong Gil Dong, one of the most brilliant operations of the Vietnam War. I only recently discovered the incredible story about the crucial role of Jeong's dreams in the success of this operation. Jeong dreamt that he caught a prisoner of war but panicked because he had no rope to secure him. Taking the dream as a warning, the next day he made sure to carry a parachute cord with him, and just as in the dream, he caught a prisoner of war. Upon interrogation, the prisoner revealed the location of a nearby cave where they were storing weapons. With that valuable information, we were able to track down the cave and seize about 980 enemy weapons—a very rare find.

The prisoner in that story is also mentioned in General Chae's memoir, 'The Vietnam War and I,' as well as in 'Testimonies of the Vietnam War and the Korean War 2' by the Ministry of Defense, in the chapter written by Lt. General Chan-Ki Min.

Because each writer tells the story from his point of view, the details may differ slightly, but all the records point to a single, historical event.

The message that President Jeong wants to convey through this book is this: "God will honor and reward the deeds of the one who cherishes life on the battlefield." Achieving victory in even the fiercest of battles without killing the enemy, and capturing the enemy but sparing his life: this, in itself, is a miracle in war, and I firmly believe in Jeong's message—no other explanation can suffice.

Until that time, people's opinion of me bothered me a lot. They often said, "He cared excessively for his subordinates above all else." However, that incident wiped away their criticisms and resolved all my silent frustration.

The Vietnam War Research Society, a group of active, junior military officers, arranges reunions among Vietnam War veterans, allowing the 3rd company soldiers to meet regularly. Last month, about ten of us were telling stories of Commander Chan-Ki Min, when a former communications officer mentioned how the commander called Jeong, "the son of God" several times. The story of this name comes up later in the book, but I found the encounter so serendipitous that I wanted to briefly share.

It was during the memorable operation at Honba Mountain. Jeong was part of the advanced guard/front line unit, and after completing that incredibly dangerous mission, he and another soldier took a break to bathe in a small pool. As they were doing so, two Vietcong soldiers fired at them from hiding, but didn't hit them. Their guns had somehow misfired, and both Jeong and the other soldier survived. This miracle came to light that night when the two Vietcong surrendered and told Commander Min about it.

Another time, we had conducted a six-day search operation without success, so the commander ordered a re-rummage operation to find at least one grenade. Jeong went ahead of everyone else and discovered an enemy grenade, but just as he picked it up, he felt somebody smack him in the back of the head. The grenade was live, but the blow sent it flying from his hand and landing in a small rock crevice, so not one soldier was hurt or injured. The unbelievable part of the story, though, was that no one was behind Jeong at the time. The platoon leader also mentioned this story in his autobiography. I really believe that President Jeong must be the son of God. If the grenade had exploded at that time and injured or killed any of the men in the 3rd battalion, 1st platoon, Commander Min would have been held responsible for the incident.

Jeong's second tour of Vietnam was just as impressive as his first, in his role as M79 grenade launcher specialist with 3rd Company, 1st Platoon, 2nd Squad. On his return to Vietnam after six months in Korea between tours, he was devastated to learn that his company had suffered high casualties without him. Always trusting that God was with him, Jeong willingly took part in more than 300 battles over the course of his two deployments. He participated in 70 extremely dangerous, high-risk operations, serving as an advance guard, a sergeant, a platoon leader and a courier. Through this, I hope you will be able to understand the degree to which this man loves and values the lives of all people.

President Jeong believes that the training he went through in battle equipped him with the strength and power he would later use to testify for God. Jeong was awarded numerous medals for his accomplishments, but the administering body at the time was not able to properly grant those medals, which I mention so that future generations reading this will not misunderstand. As a high-ranking military official at the time, I am in a position to recognize these accomplishments, even though it is late, and so I wish to accredit President Jeong with all honor, gratitude, and merit for his service. Perhaps this strong desire has led me to give a bit too much detail.

Internationally, academic studies of war have reached the conclusion that an army should aim to reach its goals with as little sacrifice of life as possible, and that war should be won 'by default' and should be 'fought indirectly.' These experts have recognized the blind cruelty of war and have advocated an approach that is more conscious and respectful of human life. I believe this book shows the way this can be achieved in future world conflicts.

17

President Jeong's book, 'War was cruel. Love and Peace,' aligns with this movement towards respect for life even during war. I believe this book will become the philosophy, the guide book, and the testimony to lead us into a world without war, and I highly recommend people read it.

When this book is published, I hope that the corruption mentioned in its pages will be completely resolved, along with the remaining misunderstandings that exist in our society. I am encouraged to hear that Jeong's fighting style is analyzed and used in military educational books, as an example of mental strength.

In conclusion, I believe this book will remind a generation that has forgotten the realities of war of the cruelty and danger found therein. I hope that this book will become a guiding light to lead this world, still so desperately in need, along the path of love and peace.

I pray for the continued health and safety of President Jeong and finish here.

October 2017, a comrade from Chilgok, Daegu

An honest soul; a man who desperately searched for God on the battlefield and risked his life in the pursuit of peace and love

PLATOON LEADER
(COLONEL OF THE RESERVE FORCES) | *Hee-Nam Choi*

About 45 years ago, I served in the Vietnam War as the Commander of the 1st Platoon, 9th Division, ROKA (Republic of Korea Army): 28th Regiment, 1st Battalion, 3rd Company. In the nearly half-century that has passed, those memories have grown misty like faded photographs. Nevertheless, there is one operation that clearly comes to mind whenever I think of the Vietnam War.

The operation, known as 'Operation Hong Gil Dong,' was the second military-level operation conducted by Korean troops in Vietnam, and was considered to have had the greatest impact on the stabilization of the region. The highlight of the operation was the 1st Platoon's successful destruction of the headquarters unit of the 95th Regiment of the North Vietnamese Forces (the Vietminh). It was achieved through intense conflict.

In those critical stages, the only way to survive was to destroy the enemy. However, in the midst of that cruel struggle of life and death, one of our platoon members managed to capture an enemy soldier, and the prisoner happened to be the batman for the commander of the North Vietnamese forces. Information revealed during interrogation about the Vietminh's strategic condition and the terrain enabled us to carry out the operation successfully.

The story of capturing this prisoner of war during that operation is so well known that it was discussed in both General Chae's memoir, 'The Vietnam War and I,' and 'Testimonies of the Vietnam War and the Korean War 2,' published by the Ministry of Defense.

The platoon member who risked his life that day to take a Vietminh prisoner of war is, in fact, the author of this book, President Jeong. It was very rare to take prisoners at the time. Every battlefield was a storm of bullets, and capturing an enemy meant risking one's own life. The difficulties of dealing with prisoners afterwards further increased the general reluctance of most soldiers to take prisoners.

At the time, I asked him, "Why did you take the Vietminh soldier prisoner instead of killing him?" His response was this: "True victory is not achieved by killing the enemy. Genuine peace can only exist when you are willing to cherish even the life of your enemy." At the time, I could not understand him. Loving your enemy in war and not killing him? The idea did not make sense to me.

45 years later, I happened to see a report from the United States National Defense University on 'Strategic Leadership Training for the Prevention of Future Conflict.' This report was a compilation of interviews with active

military captains and generals discussing the lessons they learned while fighting in Iraq and Afghanistan. I was quite surprised to read their conclusion: "We learned that there is no army with unconditional strength, and that victory is not something you can achieve by killing the enemy." The United States military prides itself on being the strongest in the world, and the experts mentioned in the report have fought countless battles, so it was interesting to me to see these diverse leaders in strong agreement that, "killing thousands of the enemies can never, of itself, bring ultimate victory and true peace."

Reading this immediately brought to mind the words of my fellow soldier, Myeong-Seok Jeong: the priceless lessons recently learned by experts in the U.S. Military and around the world after going through countless battles and wars for endless years were the same things Jeong had realized 45 years ago. Although his time on the battlefield was relatively short and his rank was low, he was able to clearly grasp this idea of where true victory and peace come from and act on that understanding. This shocked me and made me think deeply, and I have now come to see things in a new light.

Jeong's words and actions at that time were not those of an average person. It is abundantly clear to me now that he lived his life by the teachings of God and Jesus, whom he loved unconditionally.

Years ago, I published a memoir of my days fighting in the Vietnam War, titled, 'the Vietnam War story of my youth,' and subtitled, 'the man of God I met in the War.' That book contains many stories that center around Jeong. Though I have attended church and believed in God all my life, I have never seen or even heard of someone who loves God as genuinely and unconditionally as he does. I saw how he lived his life as we fought together, and I have never seen anyone put faith and love for God into action the way that he does.

I was delighted to hear that President Jeong was publishing a book about his time in the Vietnam War and even prouder to hear the title: 'Love and Peace in the Midst of a Cruel War.' As I hold this book in my hands, his face appears vividly in my memories. On that bloody battlefield, he was absolutely fascinated by God and Jesus and put his love into action every day. Those days we fought side by side, riding the rollercoaster of life and death, all come to mind.

The memories are still vivid: a simple looking young man, with a small build and innocent face. He always carried a Bible next to his heart, and whenever there was a free moment, he would pull it out to read it and pray. Even during short break-times in battles, he would diligently write notes. In the Vietnam jungle, where the air was so hot it felt like it could even cook your skin, he would share his water with his comrades. That water was more valuable than blood. Whenever there were difficult situations or operations, he would always volunteer himself and quietly carry out the work. I'll never forget Jeong's pure heart and trustworthiness.

This book brings to life what the battlefield was like for soldiers fighting on the frontlines, with detailed stories of the experiences platoon members went through. In the danger of war, where it was difficult to see what the future held even one step ahead, Jeong desperately sought God and risked his life to practice love and peace on the battlefield. This is a compelling story of the incredible history God made through him.

Both General Yeon-Woo Jeong and General Chan-Ki Min (now deceased), serving as company commanders at the time, loved and trusted Jeong more than anyone else. They both directly witnessed the way God worked through him and would have been thrilled to hear about this book.

After living out his philosophy of 'loving lives' in the Vietnam War, Jeong has now become a highly respected religious leader, teaching thousands of people around the world about the love of Christ. In that struggle between life and death, he obeyed the word of God with his life on the line, and he truly believed peace would follow if he loved first. With this conviction, he loved and cherished even the lives of his enemies: this is the faith with which he has lived his life until now. As a comrade who fought with him and as his platoon commander, I can clearly and confidently testify to all these things.

I really wanted you to know a little more about Myeong-Seok Jeong before you begin to read this book, so my testimony has grown a bit long. He is a man of great fidelity, who loyally served his country and his people, as well as a sincere man of faith. If you know the kind of man he is, you will truly be moved and inspired by the contents of this book. Under those blue skies, during the burning hot days of our youth, we fought together, enduring the inexorable forces of life and death. To President Jeong and my Vietnam War comrades, may God bless you in everything.

November, 2012 at Gaepo-Dong. A former comrade.

Hee-Nam Choi

A book written through the inspiration and wisdom granted to me by the Almighty, my savior.

Someone who has never experienced war can never truly understand how a person feels and acts in such an environment. They cannot know what it is like to fight with one's life on the line, climbing over the corpses of fellow soldiers with the smell of blood in one's nostrils, or trapped beneath the dead bodies of the enemy. The words and judgement of someone who has never experienced war cannot sit well in the heart of someone who has experienced it.

In the 1960s, I served two tours of the Vietnam War in order to defend my nation's position, alleviate the suffering of a neighboring nation, and promote my country's international standing by pursuing peace and freedom as a Korean soldier. I wrote this book honestly based on what I saw, felt, and experienced.

As someone with no expertise writing about war, I was not able to express myself with exciting phrases and flowery language. However, I wrote this book based on my own experiences and actions as a combat soldier so that it would be realistic. I hope it helps you understand the reality and the position of Korean soldiers who fought in the Vietnam War or the Korean War, and how they fought.

This book was not written to show the cruelty of war or to be interesting in the way a novel might attract many readers. While I have also addressed the issues of war and life, I have written this book focusing on the way God works in secret and the miraculous ways He helped me avoid death.

If someone had asked me to write this book, I would not have done it. In that battlefield, where I faced death again and again, it was God who saved me each time. God inspired me to write this book when I expressed my gratitude and thankfulness for His grace. Indeed, my conscience would not allow me not to write it. In addition, when I shared these stories with various people, those who were touched encouraged me to write a book.

It was difficult for me to remember the details of things that happened more than 45 years ago, even when I read back over the journals I had written at the time. Nor was it possible to find all my fellow soldiers and write the book with them.

Nevertheless, I was greatly assisted by data from certain Vietnam veterans, which helped me to write in more concrete detail. In particular, General Yeon-Woo Jeong and General Chan-Ki Min, who were my company commanders at that time, helped me by sharing many stories before they passed away.

I was very fortunate to listen to the stories of the Vietnam War again from my platoon leader, now a colonel, Hee-Nam Choi, and Colonel Pan-Yong Jang, when I was stuck writing. The soldiers I fought alongside who are still alive and healthy also gave invaluable assistance. Thank you all.

Most of all, I wrote this book about the war because the Almighty saved me, gave me wisdom, and inspired me. I think this must be the same for everyone, but writing a book really makes your black hair turn grey and your body become stiff and rigid. I started writing this book in 1999, and I threw out the manuscript several times along the way.

However, since I could not turn away from the One who saved me, I spent eight years writing it with tears, and read and revised it for a further ten years. Telling stories comes easily to me, but writing a book is very difficult. It also took longer because of my work as a representative of Heaven: the work of peace and salvation around the world.

I have written this book to enlighten you to the will of God, which was to protect the lives of many people through me, though I am just one person. Unlike other books, this book will help you realize how God protects your life and what God wants for you. Rather than making you feel the fear and terror of war, this book will make you realize more about life.

I faced combat many times in my two tours of Vietnam, but after decades had passed, I could not remember the details of all those occasions, so I have written only what I remembered, even though I still feel like something is lacking. Still, I would like to reiterate that I wrote this book because it was God's will to speak through the experiences and realizations of one person and thus enlighten all people.

Hating and fighting against another person is the same as going into battle with them, even if you don't threaten them with a knife or gun. I truly hope that this book will become your weapon to prevent such war from taking place even in your heart.

I also want to sincerely thank everyone who labored day and night to get this book published.

June, 2018

Author, Myeong-Seok Jeong

Training in a special training ground at the foot of Yongmun Mountain

IN THE VIETNAM

PATH OF A SOLDIER

WAR 1966-1969

"I crossed over Seonghwangdang hill from my hometown, Wolmyeongdong, to Jinsan, and from there I headed to Nonsan boot camp. It was February 23, 1966, the year I turned 21."

CHAPTER 1

PATH OF A SOLDIER

BEFORE ENTERING THE MILITARY

Three days after receiving the draft notice, I left home to join the army. That morning, the rain was pouring down as my mother walked me as far as the Wolmyeongdong village well. She gripped my hands tightly in hers and said, "Stay healthy until you return."

With an anxious heart, she choked out a farewell. "Don't worry about things back at home. Write often. There's only pain after you leave here."

I thought of how hard my mother always worked, and how much harder she would have to work after taking my responsibilities on top of her own. That made me anxious and teary too, like something heavy pressing on my chest. "Mom, don't worry. They give us food and clothing in the army, so life will be easier than at home, and I won't have anything to worry about. When they start paying me, I'll send you money every month."

Who would have guessed that this body of mine would end up heading for the battlefields of Vietnam?

34

I climbed the Seounghwangdang trail from my hometown of Wolmyeong-dong to Jinsan village, and from there I headed to Nonsan for training. It was February 23, 1966, and I was 21 years old.

All of us soldiers did six weeks of basic training at Nonsan, and then I did three weeks training at Geum-ma before being assigned to a unit and sent to Gangwon province. After some time in the reserves, I was transferred to my permanent station.

*After six weeks of initial training in Nonsan, we were sent for three weeks of special infantry training at another location.

*AUGUST 27TH, 1966 WHITE HORSE REGIMENT FAREWELL EVENT

IN THE VIETNAM

BEFORE BEING DEPLOYED TO VIETNAM

WAR 1966-1969

"As a believer of God,
don't you think you should
go there first before anyone else
and help stop the fighting?"

CHAPTER 2

BEFORE BEING DEPLOYED TO VIETNAM

THE FEAR OF WAR

I belonged to the 9th Army Division, White Horse unit, and was initially stationed at the base of Yongmun mountain in Yangpyeong, Gyeonggi Province. On our left shoulders, we all wore the galloping White Horse signifying our division. After being assigned to the White Horse, I was informed that I would receive further training that was specific to my unit. We were all required to master various individual combat techniques and followed a grueling weekly training regime that included overnight sessions.

Other soldiers who came and went from our training location said that our unit had been chosen for active duty in Vietnam, to which we cautiously responded that it was bad luck to spread rumors and that such an idea was 'ridiculous.' Nevertheless, we wondered aloud whether they were really just empty words. When we asked our officers directly, they lied to us saying that other units were being sent out, and our unit was not, so that we wouldn't be afraid.

However, the training they put us through was nothing like regular training. Ours was intense special combat training both day and night, so the smarter soldiers quickly figured out that our unit was indeed being deployed. Our commanders started losing sleep over the possibility of deserters since they would be held responsible and face severe reprimand for any such incident.

Even after the first training camp in Nonsan and the second training camp in Geum-ma, they continued to put us through exhausting training in preparation for being sent into combat. Our commanders told us that a drop of sweat in training would save us a drop of blood in the war, and they fiercely drilled us around the clock.

Training was one thing, but terrifying rumors about Vietnam were worse. The most fearful topic was the traps dug everywhere by the Vietcong. More than two meters deep, these pits were lined with barbed wire or sharpened bamboo spears smeared with cow dung, which would stab anyone who fell in and cause their flesh to rot. These nightmarish booby traps were said to be so common that even a ghost couldn't avoid them during night operations. Rumors like these flew around the training camps from mouth to mouth.

Many soldiers were afraid of going to war and wondered whether they would live or die, and I later found out that the 9th Division had overall desertion rates of over 60 conscripts per day. When people are actually dealing with an issue, they often find it's not as bad as they expected. However, the fear of something terrible happening in the future can produce extreme anxiety and stress even to the point of severe pain or shock, so the terrorized person feels like his bones are disintegrating or like his heart has been struck by lightning.

Among the soldiers experiencing this pain, those with money or connections sent urgent letters to families or friends, looking for any way to avoid going to Vietnam. People said that with money, one could even buy life, and truly, they were seeking to buy their own lives.

I had no one to rely on except God in whom I believed, so I made my petition to Him, "O, God! I have no money and no one to look after me in the world. So please be my 'friend in high places' and pull me out of here so I don't go to the battlefields of death. If You save me, I will bring many lives back to You, God!" Since I evangelized so much and was a faithful worker in the church, I felt like God would take me out of the group that was being sent to Vietnam. Full of this hope, I made up my mind to train hard, since the training could be useful in other ways even if I didn't go to war.

However, the longer I waited, the less it seemed like God would pull me out of the war. I had really thought that I, of all people, wouldn't have to go to Vietnam, but as my hope evaporated, I thought to myself that perhaps God wasn't able to use his power unfairly. When it seemed that nothing else would work, I thought perhaps the best strategy was to get sick, so that my name would be taken off the list of soldiers going to war.

The Vietnamese climate was tropical, up to 40 degrees Celsius; the Vietcong materialized from the jungle like ghosts to snatch away lives; terrifying booby traps dug at random and fitted with spears would kill or maim any who fell into them; venomous insects could deliver death with one bite; the jungle was full of harsh and poisonous plants... When I thought about the environment in which we were expected to fight, the fear of death and of such horrors caught my heart.

When I look back, God, the Holy Son, and the Holy Spirit protected me so that I was able to complete my active duty and return safely; however, not knowing that at the time, I brought suffering on myself with those wrong thoughts. Indeed, there is nothing more tragic than ignorance. People go through the suffering of hell both physically and for eternity in spirit due to ignorance of God's heart, ignorance of the world, and ignorance of themselves. To know is to reach a divine level.

I wasn't the only one afraid of going to Vietnam; the other soldiers shared the same heart. It turned out that only one out of the 180 members of our company had volunteered to go to Vietnam. I wondered if he was especially patriotic, but it turned out he was an orphan who didn't care much for his own life. You could say that he was strong and brave to overcome the loneliness he must have felt, but other than him, no one in the company had volunteered to go.

Our commanders stirred up our curiosity by telling us that we could earn more money in a month in Vietnam than in two years in Korea, and that we could return wealthy and buy a house, as long as we came back alive. So, the money was one thing, but on the other hand, none of us liked the idea of leaving behind our loved ones – parents, siblings, wives, children, girlfriends – and anyway it would all be in vain if we died.

War instilled in us a great fear of death. I was also deeply anxious, and in the grip of that fear, I prayed to be taken off the list of soldiers being sent to the war – that world of death.

"YOU SHOULD GO THERE AND STOP THE FIGHTING"

Around that time, I started to get sick. At first, I thought I had eaten some spoiled food, as I had the runs. I expected I would feel better in a few days. But as days passed, my fever got worse, and I became unbearably sick. It made me happy, initially, because I thought it was a sign that God was getting me out of the war, so that hope helped me to put up with the pain.

But after a few more days, it was so bad I couldn't take it anymore and had to tell the squad leader that I was too sick to take part in the mountain training that day. Afraid that I would abscond, he told me I didn't need to train but had to go with them, and I could lie down there. However, I hadn't eaten for days, and I was even too dizzy to follow them to the training site. Seeing that I was too exhausted and couldn't train, the squad leader left me in the barracks.

I was sick constantly and was suffering so much I thought I was going to die, even drifting in and out of consciousness. For about ten days, I had a fever and bloody stool. The thought of being too sick to go to war brought some comfort, but at the same time I worried, 'I'm so sick, am I going to die like this? It's not that God promised to make me get sick; it's just me suffering to the point of losing my mind. What if I suffer this much and still have to fight? Then it's just my own loss.' While lying in the barracks groaning night and day, I had a profound realization: 'It's better for me to die in Vietnam than die here in pain. Anyway, just because we're sent to Vietnam doesn't mean we'll all die. It's better to fight bravely for freedom, and if I survive, it can be an achievement to be proud of for the rest of my life.'

At that moment I heard a spiritual voice: "Even if no one else goes, at least you should go. Can you just walk away when your brothers are fighting and bleeding? Should you escape and just go your own way? As a believer of God, don't you think you should go there before anyone else and stop the fighting? A fight between individuals escalated and now the whole nation is fighting, and other nations have even gone there to stop them, so shouldn't you go there too? Shouldn't you go there to see and report what is happening with prayers and petitions?" The voice rebuked my conscience. He spoke to my spirit again: "Since you believe in me, don't tremble for fear of death, but lead others so there can be peace for mankind. I will be with you. Do not be afraid."

On hearing this voice, I shed endless tears of remorse and shame, and I repented until the floor where I was sitting was wet with my tears. After repenting, a fiery joy came over my heart, and I felt thrilled. Although I was still sick, the pain was gone and had been replaced with joy and strength. Truly God's thoughts had been so different from my own. I now realized that going to Vietnam was God's will for me. Since God, my God, was going to Vietnam with many other nations to stop the fighting there, I believed that the long war in Vietnam would gradually come to an end. Yes. It was true. If no one stopped the fighting, they would just keep killing each other. I felt ashamed of my fear of death and my desperate attempts to avoid going, and I repented deeply. I realized that I had made myself sick by not wanting to go to Vietnam. When my heart turned around, I felt blissful instead.

The Bible tells the story of the prophet Jonah. God told him to go to the city of Nineveh and preach His word, but Jonah was afraid, so he went in the opposite direction. As he was running away, the sea swallowed him up, and he suffered greatly. When Jonah repented and went to Nineveh to cry out God's message to the people, they all heard and obeyed, and so Nineveh became peaceful instead of suffering God's judgement. Peace came to Nineveh through the condition Jonah set, and so the most ideal result was achieved, and the story became a lesson for future generations.

I was reminded of this story and realized that just like Jonah, I was suffering because I was trying to avoid the place where God had told me to go. As long as I went there and, as a soldier, set the condition of peace, the war would end, and the world would be at peace.

When I repented and turned the direction of my heart, the fever subsided, and I began to feel better. I had lost so much weight from pretty much fasting for ten days, so right away, I got up and went to the cafeteria to eat. I made up my mind that since I had to go to Vietnam anyway, I would train harder than anyone else and go courageously.

WHEN I MADE UP MY MIND, EVERYONE ELSE FOLLOWED

The next day, I went off to training with newfound courage that overcame my lack of physical strength. My comrades, who knew how sick and exhausted I had been, asked how I had recovered so quickly, and they asked if I had made myself ill to get out of going to Vietnam.

I told all of them my experiences of the last few days and what I had realized. I said, "Can you just ignore it if you see people fighting on the street and blood being shed? Wouldn't you want to go and stop the fight? Like this, Vietnam cannot stop the bloodshed on its own, so other countries are going there to stop it, and we should do the same." They drank down everything I was saying like they were quenching their thirst with cold water.

I told them we had been chosen and were going to Vietnam whether we liked it or not, so if they tried to avoid it like I had, they would also suffer in both heart and body like I had. When I spoke to them sincerely and earnestly, they all listened and felt inspired. They started to change how they were thinking about it and said they should go too. I encouraged them that being forced to do things led to trouble, but they could easily change the way they thought about it. People can overcome many difficult things by taking action joyfully. Furthermore, I told them this was connected to the destiny of our nation, the world, and even Heaven, so God would surely help us. Finally, they all agreed that all lives were in the hands of God.

After I came to my senses, God used me to change the thoughts of my fellow soldiers. The soldiers in my platoon noticed I was smiling and looking happy and comfortable, so they were curious why I would be happy about going to Vietnam. When I told them what I had been through, their hearts also became calm, like a sailboat easing its way out to sea on the wind. Their hearts became united, and they realized there was no need to try to avoid going, as that would only bring more worries and sickness of heart.

Anxiety and worry are truly monsters that torment mankind. Stress makes even easy things fail, and worrying unnecessarily only brings on suffering of the mind, which can lead to disease or even death in extreme cases.

Chan-Ki Min, the commander of 3rd Company, called me in to see him and asked if I was a church-goer. When I said yes, he began to unload what was in his heart: "No matter how you guys try to get out of it, eventually, you all have to go to Vietnam. If you resist the training and have to be forced to go, I worry so much. As your commander, I worry about you men day and night. Since you're all going anyway, why not just accept it? Then we can all be happy. Do you think I'm going because I want to go? I really get how you feel about it – it's even worse for me because I have a wife and kids." He asked if I could try to persuade the other recruits, and said, "Let's make the best of this."

I sat there for more than thirty minutes and explained what I had experienced to the commander, who was also Christian. He listened deeply and even teared up a little. It seemed that he was surprised and inspired. Later, he encouraged me by saying that since he, the commander, was a person of faith, I shouldn't worry about the unit. He said, "I also feel reassured just knowing there are people like you." Even though it was so far back in the past, I still clearly remember that heartwarming conversation with a fellow Christian.

And so, even though the soldiers in my platoon and the whole company had wanted to escape the war just like me, when I turned my heart around, everyone else did too, and we were able to go through the training program with equanimity.

Sometime later, the government conducted a psychological survey and found that of the soldiers being sent to Vietnam, over 90% said they would volunteer to go! It was amazing to see other people going through the same turn-around I had. It was as if everyone had talked it over, and their hearts had all changed like mine. I looked up to the heavens and nodded toward God as if I had realized something. When thousands of people are lining up in a sports field, all the lines depend on the standard person they are lining up behind. If the standard person moves, the lines will not be straight, but if he is standing on the right spot, the lines will be straight. Now that I am older and more experienced, I notice if God sends me a sign through the slightest thing, like the touch of a single strand of hair on my face. But back then, I was too young and too dull to realize the divine will of God even if He were to show me something as obvious as a rock falling from the sky.

Even though some people ran around asking everyone they knew to help them avoid going to Vietnam, and even though I decided to entrust my life to God to serve him and struggled not to go, in the end, all of us had to pick up our heavy packs and guns and leave for Vietnam. God works according to what people decide in their hearts. People who are going to die will die anyway even if they don't go to war, and those who will live will survive even when bombs are exploding all around them. There is a Korean proverb that says, "A person who is going to drown will even die with their nose in a plate of water." It means that even trivial things can cause the most difficulties. Even though war was terrifying and the fear of death was like my blood draining away and my bones being broken, I made up my mind to follow the destiny of my nation and accept heaven's will. When I made up my mind in this way, I felt happy, even excited and hopeful, about going.

Sending soldiers to Vietnam was the beginning of Korea's path toward becoming an advanced nation: economically, culturally and also in terms of international diplomacy. Some have argued that South Korea fostered its reputation as a liberal democratic country and made an impression on a world stage at that time. Just as my family's financial situation improved because I went to Vietnam, my country's financial situation also improved because of all the soldiers it sent out.

TRAINING FOR VIETNAM

We began all-out training in preparation for our dispatch to Vietnam. We often returned from night training around the Yangpyeong mountain area at two in the morning. Although the training was exhausting, I would always read a few pages of the Bible before sleeping. We would get a special late night snack when we did night training, which was one small carton of milk and a bread roll or a packet of hardtack. Some people slept right away because they were too exhausted, but most of us ate first. Gosh, when I think back, I can still remember how tasty that snack was, even though it was more than 45 years ago.

It would have been so satisfying to eat two bread rolls or two packets of hardtack, but our country was too poor to feed us more at the time. It was so hard to eat just one that I really wished I could buy more bread for everyone. Perhaps because of that experience back then, I always ask people to buy food for everyone to eat as much as they want when they are following me around, so that no one feels unsatisfied. Even after everyone eats, if anyone is still drooling over the food, I give them more. In any case, even though I dearly wanted to eat more of that bread during training, I got to eat my fill of it in Vietnam.

We were forced to train through the heat-waves of May, June, and July so that we would acclimatize to the tropical heat of Vietnam. It was so hot that it was hard to breathe even standing still, but our combat training required us to walk and run. We were completely drenched in sweat. Those summers were so hot, 45 years ago.

That round of training lasted over three months, and when it was done, we went to Yongmun mountain valley for guerrilla-style ranger combat training. This involved rappelling down cliffs, climbing up cliffs, crossing rope bridges over deep valleys, riding a zipline, diving into the river, and more.

Peering over the cliff before descending made me shake so much I thought I would faint with fear. Many people enjoy rappelling so much they want to do it again, but before trying it the first time, we were all afraid. Riding the zipline across the river made me feel like I was in a circus performance. I got chills down my spine. That training gave us the courage and confidence that we could do anything, and it trained me to jump from high places and land like a leopard.

| Rock climbing |

For example, the single rope bridge maneuver required us to lay flat on a rope stretched across the valley and to shuffle across it by pulling on the rope. The instructors used to shake the rope when a soldier got about half way across, making anyone with less upper-body strength fall off and hang upside down like a piece of barbecued pork. Since it wasn't possible to climb back onto the rope, they had to cross the remaining distance upside down.

Luckily for me, I was good at single rope bridge training. However, rappelling down a cliff while holding onto a rope was truly a struggle. It was so scary that I just couldn't face it. I tried to hide from the instructors to get out of doing it, but one of them caught me. I told him that just looking at it made me dizzy and I couldn't do it, but he just shouted at me to hurry up and get on with it. 'It's more fun to go down the rope than to walk down,' he said. I had to do 20 bunny-hops as punishment and then rappelled down on the rope. Actually, it was fun.

At the time, I felt a bit resentful toward the instructors, questioning whether they really needed to push us that much. However, through all the training I did at that time, I developed my body into a weapon to protect myself and others, and I was able to use the skills I gained not only during the war but throughout my life. These days, some people even pay for this kind of training because they want to be strong. Many things are scary or incomprehensible the first time we encounter them, but as time passes and we mature, we become more capable of understanding and even look back positively on those memories. Army training makes some people blindly obedient because it trains soldiers to yield to their superiors, but it wasn't like that for me. If there was something I had to do anyway, I tended to take the lead and go forward before being asked. I felt happier being proactive, and the task didn't seem as hard.

We did so many drills in ranger training. Around every corner was an instructor waiting with a club to hit anyone who slacked off or to make us do push-ups. Sometimes they hit us just to make us more alert, or gave us basic punishment drills like bunny hops or 'Wonsan bombing' (planking with feet and head on the ground, butt in the air and hands behind the back). People often say that military instructors punish trainees without reason, but the disciplinary punishment we went through in ranger training was like mental training to prepare us to do more dangerous drills without any accidents. The soldiers always complained about the punishments and threatened things like, "That bastard is gonna end up half dead if he crosses my path once I get out of the army." But it was just a way of blowing off steam. After everything was over, it became part of our life stories.

In this way, the ranger training was especially designed to train our minds, because even a momentary loss of alertness could lead to an accident or death. You can do practically anything if you're alert. Even 45 years later, I still remember that training when I'm climbing mountain cliffs with people following me, and even just seeing any old rope makes me wish I could once again cross a single rope bridge. All that training became such a source of strength for me in my own life and when leading other people around the world. It is worthwhile for all men to do such drills. These days there are ranger training drills and exercise courses that people can do to develop endurance and feel a thrill at the same time.

After more than three months of training in Yangpyeong near Yongmun mountain in Gyeonggi Province, with just two weeks remaining before we left for Vietnam, our gear was inspected. We had to lay out all of our supplies on a military poncho on the training field to see whether we still had everything we had been given. I was surprised to realize there were more than 80 items on the poncho. We often had to do emergency drills where we loaded up with all our gear and equipment to set out to fight.

When all our training was complete and the day came to depart, they told us the exact route we would take to Vietnam. We walked to Yangpyeong Station, travelled by train to Yongsan Station, took the military truck waiting for us there, and gathered at Yeouido Airport. Then we marched the city streets for the farewell ceremony. After that, we went by train from Yeongdeungpo Station to Busan and took the troopship waiting off the coast to Vietnam.

| AFTER TRAINING, OUR BAGS WERE CHECKED AT YANGPYEONG |

THE FAREWELL CEREMONY

It was morning on the day we left for Vietnam. The dawn sky was particularly dark. People of all ages, from grandparents to young children, came from the Yangpyeong mountain area with lamps to bless us on our departure. Lining the streets, they urged us tearfully to be safe and return alive. These were the same sentiments of our parents and families back at home, and they pressed our hands and embraced us just as our families had. "Please come home alive," they begged, to which we put on a brave face and said, "We had excellent training, so we will fight well and return safely!" Our bold attitude seemed to give them comfort, and cries of "Hurrah, White Horse Division!" echoed through the mountains.

In fact, over the course of the training, we had caused a lot of damage to crops and had bothered the locals day and night with our shouting and military songs echoing off the mountains and being audible all over town. However, they farewelled us with so much affection, as if they had forgotten everything and were imagining their own children training in their fields and marching off to war. All of them wished us a safe return and expressed their heart-felt love.

We couldn't help but cry on feeling such a strong connection with the towns-people, as if they bid us farewell on behalf of our own parents, brothers, and sisters back home. You could say that this abundant 'jung' (affection) and love for strangers is one of the unique characteristics of my people.

We arrived at Yangpyeong station as dawn broke. Suddenly, family members, government officials from the town, and other citizens were crowding around like clouds gathering in the sky. The Yangpyeong high school band played an uplifting tune to bolster our morale.

Do you know that name? The invincible men

The brave White Horse warriors, whose merits are brilliant

Holding the flag, the crusade of justice, bearing it high

There is justice wherever the White Horse goes.

The White Horse is running to the land of Vietnam,

Come back alive, warriors of Korea.

- Military song 'Run, White Horse' -

We hadn't even been to Vietnam, but we were already getting consolation letters, right there on the spot. Some people were looking for love and fell in love so fast you could use the Korean expression, 'like roasting beans with lightning and eating them.' After exchanging letters, many of them started dating and even got married.

The rain cleared, and the sun broke through brilliantly that morning in Yangpyeong when we took our last look at the Yongmun mountain and the town that embraced us during that three months of training. We said good-bye to everyone and got on the train to Seoul. The windows of every railcar were open, and we waved Korean flags to the farmers as we passed them in the fields, and they stopped work to wave back. Seeing that we were soldiers on our way to Vietnam, they raised both fists and shouted, "Hurrah, White Horse!"

When we arrived at Yongsan station in Seoul, families had again gathered like clouds. A military truck was waiting for us to take us to Yeouido airfield. Yeouido wasn't much of an airfield at the time, but more of a sandy plain that covered everything in dust when the wind blew. When we arrived there, we rehearsed for marching around Seoul and greeting the president. At night, we were entertained by famous actors, singers, and comedians, and they showed films on the big screen to boost the morale of the departing soldiers as much as possible.

We were allowed to have visitors at Yeouido, so my father travelled in from our hometown. My older brother In-Seok and his wife came too – she was a talented cook, born in Gwangju, a city famous for good food, and she brought bulgogi (marinated beef), chicken, rice cake, and other things, like she was preparing a holiday feast. Even just looking at a table of food made me feel full, after eating only army rations for the last few months. The spicy kimchi gave me energy and vitality. We talked for an hour about many things and enjoyed our food.

Even though I was leaving with tens of thousands of other soldiers, my father was deeply worried about me and urged me to return safely. He acted as though he was seeing me for what could be the last time. He looked up toward heaven and said, "Life is in God's hands. But you still need to make every effort to be careful."

| BEFORE LEAVING FOR VIETNAM IN AUGUST 1966. WITH HIS FATHER AND OLDER BROTHER IN YEOEUIDO, SEOUL |

My older brother liked to play the role of the father of faith in our family, so whenever we gathered, he started preaching. I told him how I realized that it was Heaven's will for me to go to war, so I was not afraid of death or anything and was content to go. He said, "Don't worry, but fight for peace since God is with you. I'm sure you will do well and return." In-seok and my father were happy that I didn't seem too worried. Indeed, a truly happy life is to live without unnecessary worries, concerns, and anxiety.

The farewell parade for the White Horse Corps was held on August 27, 1966, at the Central Government Complex Square (now Gwanghwamun Square). We reported to the president and then marched the streets of Seoul from the Square to Ahngukdong and Jongno all the way to Dongdaemun. Citizens lined the streets like clouds, cheering for us. In that moment, fear, war and death were far from us.

As we marched along, some people jumped out to grasp our hands, give us gifts, or even give love letters. Indeed it is a person's wit, prudence, and wisdom that carry them through life, moment to moment. Even though people were standing by to keep order, women still jumped into the parade to embrace their lovers and share what felt like their last moments together. It was quite sad to watch them. She would make him promise to come back alive, and he would make her promise not to look at other men while he was gone. In the face of war and death, their emotions and the expression of their hearts were genuine and unencumbered by embarrassment.

As we marched through those streets, the citizens of Seoul showered us with paper confetti like snow. Their farewell to the departing soldiers was both enthusiastic and wholehearted.

| AUGUST 1966, SEOUL, WHITE HORSE UNIT MARCHING THROUGH THE CITY |

| Seoul stadium, called Dongdaemun stadium prior to being demolished |

Koreans are passionate and emotional people. If their hearts are touched, they will treat you so well and give you almost anything, but when things go wrong, they can just as easily turn around and slander or curse you until they are out of breath.

After such a farewell, we really had no choice but to fight bravely and return victorious as warriors of liberty and peace. Through their heartfelt love, our morale soared high.

From what my comrades said, it was the first time most of them had ever seen the streets of Seoul. Some of them hoped to live there after returning from Vietnam and being discharged. It was the first time in Seoul for me too. I can't deny I was from the countryside when I remember the awe I felt on seeing the grandeur of Seoul from the 1960s era.

The parade ended in Dongdaemun Seoul Stadium where we removed our packs and ate our packed lunches. There too, citizens covered the stadium in waves, and we were free to meet our families. After all the events for the day were finished, we were packed into military trucks and carried back to the camp at Yeouido.

The next day was a dinner and a final military inspection prior to leaving. We took trucks to Yeongdeungpo Station and boarded a steam train.

The last meetings soldiers had with loved ones there were as short as lightning strikes. What they couldn't express in words, they exchanged in letters. I looked out of the train and saw people running here and there, frantically searching for a son, brother, or lover. The soldiers inside the train were doing exactly the same. However, the train had no mercy for anxious hearts. The whistle blew and it began moving slowly, cutting off all those precious moments. People pressed their faces to the windows and sobbed, and others waved until the train was completely out of sight and far beyond their reach.

A farewell

Makes tears fall

Makes people cry

Yet, will tears and sobbing

Resolve the sorrow and worry

In the hearts of those

sending their beloved ones to war?

In this moment I pray

To the Almighty, God of life

Please, bring us back alive

Everyone shares

This anxious, pleading heart

But only those who pray to the God of life

Seem to rest easy

The train was soon speeding along. It was 8:00 pm on August 28, 1966. The soldiers stashed their packs on the luggage racks and sang or even danced, trying to distract themselves from whatever was preying on their minds. Our mood kept changing as the passing scenery changed.

We arrived at Daejeon station in the middle of the night and were greeted by a crowd of Daejeon citizens. Mothers and fathers cried out for their sons, trying to catch a last glimpse before we departed. Some couldn't find their sons even after shouting their names from one end of the platform to the other — the whole scene was chaos and also somewhat distressing. No one could hear their family members properly because of all the noise. There were mourning mothers, wives beating the ground, and even soldiers crying at the shock of leaving those they loved. Like icicles hanging from the eves melting on a spring day, our hearts melted and tears dripped down our faces, and the sound of sobbing spread from one person to the next. Holding back tears at such a moment was extremely difficult.

People from different regions had distinctly different ways of dealing with their grief: those from Seoul or Gyeonggi province shed tears like melting ice, people from Jeolla province sobbed loudly like water boiling in a cauldron, while those from Gyeongsang province didn't hold back but sobbed with the intensity of burning gasoline. People from Chungcheong province tended to hold in their tears until later, but once they started to cry, they would weep for a whole day, like a widow who had lost her only son.

There's a song that says, "Shall I sing a farewell that chokes me up? Shall I turn and shed tears of blood?" It was that kind of farewell: heading off to war with desperate feelings in our hearts. Those scenes were so sad. Who could put that grief in words? The best I can do is leave a simple record of what we saw and felt in those bitter and sorrowful moments.

Fortunately for me, I avoided the heartache of saying goodbye to my parents because they didn't come. I didn't have a wife or girlfriend either, so I wasn't feeling as anxious as those who did. Still, just watching those around me felt like crying a river of tears in my heart, and in the end I couldn't keep them inside and cried just like everyone else.

When the whistle sounded and the train began to pull away, citizens and family members who had come to bid us farewell cried out at the top of their lungs. Those saying goodbye to their lovers wept especially noisy farewells, or they turned away to hide their tears from each other. The sight of their agony touched me deeply.

The whistle sounded again, and the train moved off, unable to delay our arrival at the next destination. Several hours later we arrived at Daegu station.

| PEOPLE BIDDING FAREWELL AT DAEGU STATION |

Even though it was after 2am, the people of Daegu had come out to greet us. The people of Gyeongsang province are famous for being highly emotional. They spoke passionately, as if confirming their stereotype. They spoke so fast it was hard for me to follow the local dialect, but the Gyeongsang soldiers understood well.

The train stopped at each station for only a moment, and the only way to find a particular person was to do it at lightning speed. So each time the

| AT THE PORT OF BUSAN, SOLDIERS BOARDING THE SHIP BOUND FOR VIETNAM |

train stopped, people crowded to the windows, passing in big and small bags of gifts. They treated us as if they would never see us again.

Whether people were wailing because they couldn't find the ones they were looking for or just wailing, the train blew its whistle again and pulled away from the station. We arrived in Busan at dawn, and, shouldering our packs and picking up our guns, we began to board the ship anchored at Pier 3. The USS Gaffey was an 18,000-ton troop transport ship that had apparently transported American troops during WWII.

On August 29, after boarding the ship and being assigned sleeping quarters, I went up on deck to see the view of the beaches. It was my first time visiting Busan. The city was laid out alongside the beach like the spine of a cutlass fish.

The ship was equipped with performing stages, entertainment, and sports facilities. We were allowed to roam the ship freely since it wasn't possible to escape. After selecting a bunk, we could shower — it felt so refreshing to wash off all the dust and sweat of the journey. We felt ready for anything.

On August 30, looking down at Busan City from the deck 20 meters up felt like standing on top of a five or six-story building and made the shore feel much further away than just 150 meters. It was a beautiful clear morning in Busan harbor.

Clear blue sky

Clear blue water

Clear blue uniform

Clear blue heart and mind

Training completed

Warm farewells

And best wishes

From the people

In every city

Passing through

Now

All that remains is

Fight well

Keep the peace

Fight against those who fight against us

The fight between good and evil

Plays out all over the world

Who is good?

Who is evil?

You have to fight to know.

Sometimes the good loses

Sometimes the evil prevails

Sometimes the good dies

Sometimes the evil lives.

Still, despite all that

In the end

The evil comes to ruin
The good blossoms and bears fruit

Everyone hopes to return alive
But not everyone will live
Nor will everyone die

As if predestined
Death waits for some
It waits for them on the battlefield
Ah!
Who wouldn't want to return alive?
Who would want to die there?

The God of Heaven knows
Who will live to return
Who will die there
But He does not say

Don't tell me whether my name is included
On that list

I don't want to know

No one's fate is predestined
It depends on what you do
It is not God's will
For you to know your future
But to work hard, to rely on God
To strive and be careful
That is His will

Over the cheers of family and well-wishers, the military band played the White Horse military song and other Korean songs popular at the time, such as 'I'll return, port of Busan,' 'Goodbye Miss Kim' and 'Goodbye Miss Lee.' The sentimental music resonated around the port and in each of our hearts.

Once the sailing ceremony was completed, we cried and waved to those on shore, holding on to that last glimpse of our loved ones and our homeland. At 10 o'clock exactly, the USS Gaffey sounded its horn and suddenly, as if we had planned it, everyone dissolved in tears on the floor. People were crying both on deck and at the dockside.

Only God could see all their tears and bring them safely home from the battlefield.

DEPARTURE

Turning its back on any feelings of regret in the Port of Busan, the USS Gaffey pulled away, as if on a tight schedule, and navigated out to the open sea.

The soldiers waved their hands until Busan was no longer in sight and wiped their tears with both fists. Busan eventually disappeared over the horizon, and all those faces became faces we would not see until we returned, except in dreams or photographs.

The ship we boarded swam through the Korea Strait, passing the Taiwan Strait and the South China Sea, all the way to the land of Vietnam. When the big waves of the open sea crashed over the deck, it felt as if the ship would be buried under them. Nevertheless, that heavy lump of iron swam quite well through the high waves, carrying an enormous body of men.

The magnificence of nature, the developed brains of human beings, and the enormous warships that cross the Pacific—everything was grand and mysterious to me. Not even a minuscule speck of land could be seen. Everywhere was just water.

There were so many different kinds of fish in the vast open sea—whales, sharks, and all kinds of big and small fish. 'How sad that they might grow old and die if no one eats them,' I thought. Whenever I used to catch small mudfish living in the rice paddies, my heart would leap, and I would shout, 'Wow!' But seeing such big fish living in the ocean, I was even more excited and overwhelmed. In this way, I realized how important it is to see and experience many things, as it awakens your mind and makes you realize and learn so much.

I was mesmerized by the ocean. The water was not just one color: there were many different colors in the waves. Nature displayed its true mystery and grandeur. Truly, the magnificent sea, which occupies 70% of the earth, was made by the Creator's mysterious design. How could I have seen all this if I had not been to Vietnam? After growing up in the remote countryside surrounded by mountains, the magnificent sight of nature filled my heart with such awe and enlightenment.

If only the sea were land

I would never have lived in that small mountain valley

I would have escaped it

I would have lived in vast open spaces

The sea is immense

But what have I gained from it?

When did I ever

Have the chance to eat fish?

I envy the fishermen

Since the sea is bigger than the land

How much nicer

To live off the sea

Than by farming narrow mountain valleys

Listen, the sea calls me

'Come live in a sailboat,

Live like a god here with me'

Listen, the land calls me

'Where are you going,

How can you leave behind

Your A-frame carrier in the valleys of Wolmyeongdong?'

As the proverb says,

'A caterpillar will die from eating fallen leaves.'*

(*A caterpillar will die from eating fallen leaves: a person needs to know his place. Greed can bring misfortune.)

Ah, my hometown

Land of my youth

Where my family waits

I shall return

Even if I must float there on the sea

How can I make a new future

So easily?

Sea!

The place filled with my stories and Heaven's stories

My hometown, Wolmyeongdong

I will make it a sea

A sea of faces

- Aboard ship, en route to Vietnam

How could human beings make thousands of tons of steel swim through the oceans like a shark? One could say human understanding has reached the skies. The bunks, walls, and ceilings were all made of thick steel plates. They served us fancy Western food, which was nothing like what I usually ate. They made us clean too: there were strict cleaning inspections by American sailors, who made us keep cleaning if they found any trace of dirt or dust on the floor or walls.

Even though we were headed into battle, sailing the Pacific Ocean felt good. For a time, at least, I could eat as much as I wanted, I could freely go about on deck and watch the blue sea, the islands and the fishing boats – in short, I was delighted. It was the first time I had even been on the vast, blue sea. Many other soldiers felt the same. We admired the magnificent waters, the sharks, schools of various types of fish, and flying fish leaping as high as the waves. I was especially impressed by the array of different colors the ocean waves displayed, depending on the angle.

If this vast sea did not exist
The land would not look so beautiful

If there were no fields, no mountains big and small
The ocean would not look so beautiful

The land exists for the ocean
And the ocean exists for the land

The land is like a man
The ocean is like a woman
Nature is a match made in heaven
And through their love
The ocean gives birth to fish
And the land gives birth to animals

No human mind can fathom
The proliferation, the reproduction of nature
The creation of God

Ah! Nature's laws of existence
Are truly remarkable,
Truly mysterious, beautiful, and majestic.

Those who realize stand in awe
At the wisdom of the Creator God,
Who designed and made all this.

At night, the whole sea sparkled with the reflected light of the moon and stars. Even the moon seemed more enchanting from the sea than it had on land. Truly the moon captures the atmosphere and creates a mysterious harmony between the heavens and the earth, no matter where it is.

There were so many people on board that the line-up for food felt endlessly tedious. The benefit was that we could eat as much as we wanted.

We all ate as if it was our last meal, thinking of the war zone ahead of us. Korea, back in those days, was too poor to feed us well during training, but onboard the ship, we could eat as much as we liked. Soon, the kitchen staff complained that they were going way over the food budget. Following the philosophy attributed to Spinoza, the soldiers seemed happy to eat today even if they were to die tomorrow: "Even if I knew the world would end tomorrow, I would continue to plant my apple trees."

The trip was not just eating, drinking, and having fun, however: people started getting seasick as our speed picked up against the heavy waves. I started feeling nauseated. Soldiers vomited all over the decks, which became a new kind of hell. Some people thought they would die of seasickness before even reaching the battlefield, as they collapsed on deck. The sight of endless lines of soldiers waiting for food was replaced by the tragic scene of soldiers vomiting everywhere. Eventually, they had to reduce speed, but even that didn't help those who were particularly sensitive to motion sickness. It was like being in hell and having to spew everything out of one's stomach. No one cared about pride or rank when they were vomiting uncontrollably. I collapsed on the deck and looked with envy on those who were completely unaffected: 'Did they used to be fishermen? Wow, those bastards are ok,' I thought.

There was no guard duty while we were on board, since no one could escape off the ship. I spent a day wandering around PX (the military convenience store), the arcade, the bunks, and the deck. It was the best time to relax and do what we wanted, before the fighting started.

I preferred to wander around because lying down made me feel more nauseated. I found a rest area with a group of soldiers crowded around a vending machine. They were amazed, having never seen a vending machine before, and were enjoying the thrill of purchasing coffee, beer, soda, and so on. One soldier put money in, but when nothing happened, he cursed and kicked the machine and walked off. When a cup came out and beer was dispensed later, the guy behind him laughed at him and called him a fool for not knowing to wait, while enjoying a free cup of beer.

Another time, some pranksters filled a cup with urine and left it in the dispenser. An innocent guy wanting a beer saw it and said, "Another fool who doesn't know how a vending machine works just left without taking his beer. Idiot!" So he drank it, delighted with getting a freebie, but later he said, "American beer isn't like Korean beer – it stinks like piss."

In the end, he vomited it up, saying, "I don't think I can drink American beer." His friend got a new beer and said it was delicious. "What do you mean it smells like urine? It tastes great! Try it!" He found that his friend's beer tasted completely different. He was enraged, and I heard him shouting, "Some f-ing bastard peed in a cup and left it there. Crazy bastard. If I catch him, I'll make him eat shit!" The guy next to him replied, "Is poop scary? I told you not to drink it – I thought it was strange from the beginning. Why'd you go and drink it?"

The soldiers were full of clever pranks and mischief. Seeing them made us laugh our heads off. We hadn't had much to laugh about until then, because of the motion sickness, but those pranks had us rolling around on the deck clutching our bellies in mirth. Seeing that comical sight, I said that there are no freebies in life, and especially no free lunches – seasickness was the price we paid for our feast.

As for me, I was seasick everywhere I went: on deck, in bed, and everywhere else. There were no inspections and no one checked where we were, so I went below deck, leaving marks on doors as I passed areas where other soldiers didn't go. I ended up in the kitchen. There was so much food. The Korean kitchen police on duty asked what I was doing, and I said I was just wandering around because of the motion sickness, and he said he was feeling it too. He told me to eat whatever I wanted, eggs, turkey, etc. It all looked delicious and I ate until I was very full.

I went down to the deck below, where American sailors were going here and there and I could hear very loud machine noises. They saw me and said, "Victory!" To which I replied, "Thank you very much," and practiced my English greetings according to the time of day: good morning, good afternoon or good evening. I felt less seasick down there because the ship moved less.

I spent a few days wandering around by myself like that. The shower room was always so full of people that it was hard even to get inside, but there were less people the later at night I went, so I came up with the strategy of sleeping while other people showered and waking up at 2 a.m. to wash. I could empty out the pool and fill it up again. In the end, I was able to bathe in cleaner water. It was nice to have the whole shower room to myself, but not as much fun with no one to talk to. People feel lonely when they spend

| SEPTEMBER 5TH, 1966. ARRIVING AT THE PORT OF NHA TRANG |

too much time by themselves. In the military, they say you need to have good sense to solve problems. When I did things flexibly and sensibly, I was able to solve problems. God my shepherd led me to a place of rest and made things work out in a better way.

The high waves that made everyone seasick for two and a half days gradually subsided, and the ships also slowed down as it approached

| White Horse Unit landing, Nha Trang Port |

the destination. Everyone started feeling better, like dry plants reviving after a shower of rain.

After leaving Busan, Korea, we sailed for six days and arrived off the coast of Vietnam on the seventh day. The port was too shallow for big ships, so we transferred to landing boats for the final 500 meters and finally stepped onto the sandy beach at Nha Trang. We were welcomed into port by placards reading, 'Welcome White Horse' along with a military band and crowds of Vietnamese women.

Our nervous hearts were gripped with even more fear on hearing the far-off sounds of gunfire and explosions. They drove us to a sandy field. It was so hot that we were all breathing heavily. The sight of lizards the size of my forearm roaming around on the sand was so shocking to me that I was almost ready to faint. They told us not to worry because they wouldn't bite, but the lizards still looked so scary and gross. That was my first impression of the Vietnam War.

| PICTURE TAKEN WITH SENIOR OFFICERS IN THE UNIT AFTER
ARRIVING IN VIETNAM |

IN THE VIETNAM
WAR 1966-1969

THE DAY I GUARDED
THE FRONTLINES

"*Misunderstandings between people can be resolved through conversation and misperceptions on the battlefield can be resolved through verification.*"

CHAPTER 3

THE DAY I GUARDED THE FRONTLINES

GUN FIRED BY MISTAKE - "FRIENDLY FIRE"

We dug a moat and established a defensive position on some barren land some distance from the city of Nha Trang. That first night, I was on duty and feeling very tense. The commander ordered us to be fully alert as we scouted the 'fort.' He told us that anyone approaching from the front was an enemy, and if we didn't have time to report, we should shoot them ourselves.

At about 9 p.m., we heard loud gunshots from the direction of the enemy. Everyone was on his toes, and the whole place was on high alert. Moments after the gunfire, we received a message that two enemy soldiers had appeared and opened fire, and were seen being shot down by return fire.

An enemy engagement in the early evening meant we had no choice but to remain on alert for the rest of the night, wondering when and how many enemies would attack. We stared out at the frontline barely daring to blink. Light from the city in the distance allowed us to see even a puppy that appeared on the skyline.

Another message arrived 20 minutes later. They had checked the bodies and found the two soldiers dead of gunshot wounds. Tragically, they discovered they were Korean soldiers: a third soldier had crawled ahead of them to take a dump, and when he stood up to buckle his belt, the soldier on guard was in such a state of nervous tension that he saw movement and opened fire right away, thinking it was an enemy soldier, and killed the two soldiers. It was just a terrible accident. Nervousness killed two men.

The shooter had acted under the misperception that he was shooting at enemy soldiers, so in the end, those in command decided it was in the interest of general morale to not hold him responsible. If the soldiers who died had anticipated such a mistake, they would have stayed closer to the ground and dug a hole to do their business on the spot instead of going anywhere. It was a case of a momentary lapse leading to death. People fail or even die when they act on one piece of information without being aware of other relevant information.

We were all devastated to hear about this tragic accident on our first day in Vietnam. We were overcome with deep sorrow and grief. After all our grueling training, as soon as we arrived at the battlefront, a soldier on guard had mistaken two of his comrades for enemies and caused such horrible, meaningless deaths. For me, this incident became a permanent life lesson that I can never forget.

Afterwards, the commanding officers firmly educated us all about the attitude and mentality we needed to have. They lectured us all day that being panicky or overly nervous, even if we were facing hostility in battles, would only get both us and our fellow soldiers killed, and that we had to always check properly and act calmly. So in the end, that incident prevented other dangerous accidents being caused by carelessness. Although two soldiers died under friendly fire, it became a lesson for all of us to prevent harm to many more people.

There are many situations in life where misunderstandings or mistakes happen because we are overly anxious or doubtful of others. These mistakes often bring misfortune to both sides. Misunderstandings are like cancers that eat away at relationships. To avoid unnecessary fighting and hatred, we have to check, re-check, and resolve what was misunderstood. Like a destructive disease, misunderstanding divides families, lovers, friends, and nations, but misunderstandings can be resolved through conversation, and mistakes on the battlefield can be avoided by checking thoroughly. This life lesson was of great benefit to myself and was also something I taught those who follow me. I always taught people not to misunderstand and never to hate others.

I AM A PEACEMAKER

After a few days, our unit was transferred to another area called Kamran, where we set up camp and our home base for a few days of stay. We posted guards day and night, and underwent constant training including being educated in the events of the war up to that point. We also used the time to adapt to the tropical heat, which was often overwhelming. In Korea, farm work had included laboring under direct sunlight in extreme June heat, but Vietnam was hotter than that even when we did nothing.

After several weeks, soldiers started to collapse from heatstroke. It felt like we were fighting against the heat, rather than against enemy soldiers. The heat made it difficult to even breathe, so engaging in mountain warfare in full battle gear seemed impossible. Just the thought of it made us feel helpless.

Even while we were fighting for breath and roasting under the sun, there were some positives. One was being provided with plenty of C-rations and some of the same uniform and equipment the American soldiers used. C-rations are food rations consumed during battle (combat rations), so they included things like canned meat, fruit, biscuits, coffee, cocoa, and sugar, all in small packages. I weighed about 65kg, 5kg more than I had in Korea where food was more limited. Compared to military training in Korea with all kinds of stress and little food, roasting in the heat and fighting bravely for freedom in Vietnam wasn't so bad.

At midday, the heat was so unbearable that even the lizards didn't come out of their caves. Those lizards were about the same width as a man's forearm, and we were scared of them at first because we thought they would bite like snakes. We tried to kill them with clubs, but they were extremely fast-moving. Later we learned not only that they didn't bite but that they were actually quite friendly, and they would follow you around if you fed them.

Sometimes soldiers caught the lizards in the caves where they were hiding from the heat, and cooked and ate them. In Korea, snake meat is considered to boost virility, and they thought lizard meat would have the same effect. Regardless of what generation it is, you can't stop men from eating anything that is said to boost their virility. I was really clueless about all that, so I couldn't understand why men needed more stamina and women didn't. It gave me a headache, thinking about all the things I didn't know.

I don't know if lizard meat really had any impact on virility, but this one time, nearly all the soldiers in our unit, including those on guard duty, jumped over the wire fence and stayed out all night in a nearby town, without permission from the company leader. My job that day was to stand guard at a vulnerable post 15 meters up in a tree.

After receiving a series of education from the regiment, the company leader suddenly returned to conduct a detailed inspection of the guard. When he found out that the soldiers on guard duty stayed out all night thinking they could relax, he really blew his top, shouting and snarling like a tiger in a rage.

"Where are those little bastards?"
Unable to sit still, the company leader stalked around until he reached my guard post.

| SOLDIERS CLIMBING OVER THE FENCE AND GOING TO THE VILLAGE |

"Hey! Who is on duty up there?"

"I am Corporal Jeong from 1st Platoon."

"Where the f*** did all the soldiers of your company go?"

"I've been focusing on surveying enemy territory to the front, so I didn't see what happened behind me. I only saw a few men from 3rd Platoon going outside the wire fence to buy something."

"All those bastards went into town to hunt for women. I'm sure of it. You there, on guard, have you seen the adjutant?" He asked me, his voice loud and angry.

"No sir, I haven't."

The adjutant is the first lieutenant, the deputy company commander. Back then, we didn't have cell phones or pagers, so there was no way to contact people immediately. Eventually, the company leader told me to keep my post and yelled at the soldiers on standby to go and bring in everyone from the town, and tell them that the company leader had arrived and it was an emergency.

From the guard post, up a tree surrounded by sandbags, I turned my binoculars toward the town and looked for the soldiers. Some time after the messengers had been dispatched, the company soldiers poured out of the village, urgently crawling all over the place and sneaking back into camp through gaps in the wire fence. I was so appalled by their inappropriate behavior in a war-zone that I could barely breathe, and the hot wind didn't help, either. 'How can they fight with that kind of attitude?' I wondered, worrying if they would put all our lives at risk.

Watching through the binoculars, I saw that the soldiers coming in all had bloody noses, as if someone had beaten them up somehow. I couldn't help thinking that it was more difficult to interpret their behavior than to interpret the secrets of the Bible.

'If they went out to meet women, why would they come back with bloody noses? Did the women hit them for not spending enough money?' I wondered. Later, I found out that the nosebleeds had been caused by undercooking the virility-boosting lizards.

Soldiers share the same fate, so every time they got caught up in doing what they wanted and pleasing themselves, I was just as furious as the company leader. 'It's not the first time those scoundrels did this, and finally they got caught red-handed by the company commander himself. I bet they will get beaten until they see stars. Beating is the only way to bring sense to these psychos,' I muttered to myself, angrily. God sees everything, but I still told Him about it. I prayed for their corrupt minds to be turned around.

Soon after, the company commander's angry voice could be heard thundering across the whole camp. All the soldiers who had deserted their posts had to lie on their stomachs and be beaten. One of the team leaders who had gone into the town with them was beaten with a bedpost, while the company leader shouted at him. "Hey, you little prick! This is a war zone. Are you trying to kill your men? Is that all you learned in the army, prick?" He ordered that platoon leader to beat the soldiers in the front leaning rest position (front-leaning rest position is the top of the pushup position, widely used in the military) until they came to their senses.

After being beaten that much, the platoon leader also lost his temper and beat the soldiers who had left their post with him, shouting, "Hey, you bastards! This is a war zone. How dare you decide to just leave your posts?

Are you here to sleep around? No, you're here to fight in a war. Come to your senses, or you'll die!"

I could see everything when I came down from my post at the top of the tree. All the shouting had made me feel uneasy, so I came down to find out what was happening. Then the company commander told the platoon leader who had deserted his post to get in the 'front leaning rest' position. The platoon leader pleaded, "Let's not do this," which further enraged the company commander.

He screamed, "You little prick, you need to be educated again. Did you come here to die? Shouldn't you be on your best behavior when the company commander isn't around?"

The platoon leader answered, "I'm sorry, I'll do better." He didn't move when the company commander ordered him on the ground again, so the company commander picked up the handle of a pickaxe that was lying on the ground and struck him on the back and shoulders.

I was on good terms with both the company commander and the platoon leader, so I boldly ran up to them and grabbed the handle of the pickaxe from the company commander. He looked at me and said, "Why aren't you at your post? Get back there immediately." I replied that all the screaming and yelling had made me uncomfortable until I couldn't just stay where I was.

"Sir, I know you are furious enough to lose it, but you have to control yourself right now. Beating them won't make you feel better. Even without you hitting them, they must feel terrible. Their own consciences are pricking them like needles. I know it's upsetting, but think of how they feel and control yourself." I took the handle of the pickaxe from him and he let go of it, looking deflated.

Actually, it is quite uncommon for a soldier to stop his superior officer from beating other soldiers, but it can be done if you go about it the right way. They are adults, not children, so you have to stop them if they are angry or fighting.

At that moment, the company commander turned away from the soldiers he had been beating and looked at me. He confessed it was his own fault for not teaching those under his command properly. He wiped away tears with a handkerchief and said, "Who can I possibly blame?" Everyone else looked at him and apologized.

All the officers apologized and promised to take responsibility for their actions. "It will never happen again. Please forget everything that happened today," they begged. It seemed that everyone felt sorry for their actions.

"Since we all came here to survive together, let's all do our best. Don't you have wives and children you love back at home? Don't you want to return safely to the country that gave us birth and to the brothers who are waiting for us?" With this final exhortation, he dismissed his subordinates and then apologized to the adjutant.

The company leader, having now cooled off, gave me a firm handshake as if he were impressed that it was a subordinate who had brought about the peaceful resolution. He grinned and said, "This won't happen again, so keep an eye on me and you won't be disappointed."

Actually, it would not have been easy for him to hold back his temper after what the soldiers had done. Just a few months after arriving in Vietnam, they had lost all their alertness and become lax with security. That would be enough to make any leader shocked and worried. But if he had really lost it, unpleasantness would have lingered in the days ahead when we should have been fighting together.

After mediating between both sides and when everyone had calmed down, I returned to my guard post, deep in thought. I thanked God, realizing that God had used me as a tool to bring harmony to the unit, and I prayed that he would continue to use me in that way.

They loved,

Then their noses bled for lack of stamina.

They loved,

Then they got beaten until blood spattered.

So they saw

Stars and moon

In broad daylight.

Explosive human anger

Cannot compare

To the real explosives of war.

I stopped a bigger bomb
Stopped it from detonating
So I didn't have a chance today
To ponder and reflect,
And I wasn't aware
That the hot tropical sun had already set.

Love burns
In those men on the frontlines
But their beatings burn too.
The scorching sun also burns.
No one can block the path of fire.
No one can block the path of water.
Nor can they block
The path of love.

Ah!
The big hole in that wire fence.
No one can block that hole,
So the man standing guard
Is nervous and on edge.

From that point on, the division tightened the rules so that any soldier who jumped the fence would be dealt with by the company leader directly. Even so, the soldiers couldn't suppress their urges and continued to escape secretly by making new holes in the fence. Those who felt guilty stayed in the camp, but their thoughts went to the village all day.

Guard duty was long and tedious for the soldiers, so the subject of women often came up and provided ample distraction, sometimes right up until the replacement guard came on duty. Shamelessly, they told vivid stories of their previous exploits in the village, sniggering and laughing over their virility. I would overhear them talking, too embarrassed to listen and too curious not to. Through the binoculars that we used at the guard post I saw someone heading back to camp with his nose plugged, but when I asked why he did that and whether a woman beat him, he laughed so hard at my naïve question.

That was one of the reasons why everyone in the platoon laughed at me. There was so much I didn't know that I often said the wrong thing. My friend, Geun-Tae Yoo, explained to me that the men got nosebleeds after meeting up to eight women. So I replied that it was good they only got a nosebleed and didn't die after being beaten up by so many women. That made everyone roll around on the ground in laughter.

When they shared amusing stories about love, I would bring up stories from the Bible, but they didn't find my stories fun and would just cut me off. That made me start to think deeply about how I could share the gospel and the Bible in a fun way. When I was on guard duty, I immersed myself in the Bible, while they immersed themselves in stories of women and other worldly things.

In general, rules were very strict in the military, but they had a lenient policy toward regularly letting the men have a night out, since they had left their lovers behind and couldn't seem to control their sexual desires. It was considered that the men were young and could die any time, and therefore should be given some leeway in this area.

The village where the soldiers went, near our base, was covered in tall palm trees, giving it a tropical feel. The Vietnamese women there had small waists and dewy dove-like eyes, and they wore Ao Dai dresses with long slits up each side. Those dresses were sexier than miniskirts. When even a bit of skin was enough to turn soldiers' heads, their eyes pretty much fell out looking at those dresses. It was as if they'd been struck by the lightning bolt of love.

As for me, I was so obsessed with God and Jesus that I was clueless about the opposite sex, but those soldiers who wanted Vietnamese women left their posts constantly the entire time they were in Vietnam. I learned later that tens of thousands of part-Korean babies were born during that time.

| Tuy Hoa city at that time |

| Exercises conducted in Vietnam with the support of a U.S. helicopter unit |

In The Vietnam War 1966-1969

A MIRACULOUS CLOSE CALL
DURING HELICOPTER TRAINING

*"The day death in the sky
swallowed me but spat me out.
God, who loves me, granted me the
grace of life in the presence of death."*

CHAPTER 4

A MIRACULOUS CLOSE CALL DURING HELICOPTER TRAINING

AH~ I HAVE ESCAPED DEATH

No joy is greater than narrowly thwarting death: it is an experience you cannot forget. Likewise, there is no greater grace than rescuing a person from death. Everyone faces such near-death experiences at some point in life.

In 1967, the year following my initial dispatch to Vietnam, I was 22 years old and was a Korean soldier in the 9th infantry division, White Horse, participating in the war as a member of the allied forces. The U.S. combat plane airfield and White Horse 9th Division, 28th Regiment, Goblin Unit were located around the coast of Tuy Hòa.

The 3rd Company was called the QRF* and our job was to sweep up enemy infiltrators and safeguard the military roads connecting Tuy Hòa and Nha Trang.

*Quick Reaction Forces: a unit prepared to fight against unexpected situations and missions at all times, always carrying combat equipment and ammunition.

We were required to do several days' helicopter training on a plain near the Nha Trang coast, so that we could be sent to our operating region, Tuy Hòa. Our company in particular went through intense training, and they told us every drop of sweat in training would save us a drop of blood in battle.

That day, our training was to climb a rope ladder in midair. The whole company was 180 soldiers and each platoon of 40 soldiers were doing the training, team by team. Each seven-member team went up in the helicopter to an altitude of 300 meters, and, fully armed, each person had to climb down and back up the 10-meter rope ladder. The training was for mental discipline, for boldness and confidence, and so that we could use the rope ladder if a helicopter was unable to land due to the situation on the ground. Although you may not have done this kind of training yourself, you probably saw it on TV or in a movie.

So the helicopters were flying on rotation, east to west, while soldier after soldier climbed down and up on the rope ladder.

We were watching and waiting nervously for our turn to come. It was an anxious time for both those in the helicopters and those waiting on the ground. There was no safety belt to wear while climbing, so anyone who lost his grip would fall to his death. If you felt dizzy, you might let go without realizing, so some soldiers were telling us that closing our eyes was the best way to deal with dizziness. For other rope maneuvers a safety belt was used, but for the rope ladder, there was nowhere to attach the belt as each rung of the ladder was a different rope. The only safety belt was your own two hands gripping the ladder.

It was my first time doing helicopter training so I was pretty nervous. We hadn't done helicopter training before because it was the US helicopter unit there in Vietnam that was supporting our training.

Finally, the 1st Platoon, 2nd Squad were up, so we shook out our tense bodies and the seven of us boarded the helicopter. Inside, there were three seats in the front and three seats in the back, so one person was going to miss out on a seat. We were all looking at each other wondering who it would be, so in the end I yielded my seat and sat down on the floor. We were all nervous. "Good luck," we told each other.

The helicopter rose up toward the training altitude of 300 meters, and our squad leader was trying to figure out who would go first. Both doors were fully open, in preparation for the training. Hunkering down on the floor, I told the others to fasten their seat belts, since some of them hadn't yet.

Someone said that the training would start soon and there wasn't any point in buckling up, but I insisted that everyone except me, on the floor without a seatbelt, should be properly strapped in. The squad leader glanced around and ordered them to fasten their seatbelts, so they quickly complied. Now, it seemed safe.

I have acrophobia, so any heights make me dizzy, even swinging on a tree. The thought of climbing a rope ladder hanging from a helicopter 300 meters from the ground was utterly terrifying. 'What if I get dizzy and...?' Just the thought stole all my confidence, and on seeing the ground far below, all the blood drained from my face and I felt numb. I earnestly prayed for my safety. The guerilla training we had been through was nothing compared to this. I felt terrified and completely unprepared.

My heart was pounding at the thought of falling to my death. Everyone seemed to be thinking the same thing, because their faces were deadly pale. Various thoughts flashed through our minds, seeing the ground below through the helicopter's wide doors, none of them good. I was terrified, my fingertips were tingling and I could hardly sit still, and I kept calling out to God and Jesus in my mind, praying for protection on that dangerous exercise, for myself and my fellow soldiers.

Suddenly, without any warning, the helicopter banked 45 degrees toward the south, in the direction I was facing. I slid straight down the shiny steel floor toward the open door. I could not even scream but just kept sliding down. At that moment, I registered the cries of those in their seats.

I was crouching, a gun in my right hand and my left hand grasping nothing, sliding to my death when the heel of my combat boot caught the rail at the edge that guided the door mechanism. My center of gravity was already tilted toward the outside of the helicopter, and I was still wearing my heavy pack that weighed at least 25 kg (55 lbs.) and holding my gun. The helicopter banked sharply for 10 seconds or more, doing a U-turn.

That door rail at the edge was barely the width of a ballpoint pen, so I couldn't lean my weight on it. I couldn't even scream. I pointed my toes up with all my strength and dug in with my heel, trying to lean back into the helicopter, but it was futile: I was already overbalancing. I wanted to grab something for support but my left hand was numb and refused to respond, and there was nothing to grab anyway that would support both my weight and the weight of my pack.

I cried desperately to God and Jesus to save me. Only God could save me in that extreme emergency. I was thinking about how I could throw away my gun and pack when finally, the helicopter finished the turn and straightened up. I fell backwards and grabbed a chair leg. All my strength deserted me and I was utterly exhausted. I thought I would lose my mind and die. Then came an unwelcome beeping sound: the signal to begin the rope ladder training.

| ON THE VERGE OF DEATH DURING HELICOPTER TRAINING |

There was no way I could even think about the training or anything else, my mind was blank except for intense thanksgiving to God and Jesus.

Then anger came, and I accused my fellow soldiers, "How come you didn't grab me when I was sliding down the floor? Don't you care at all?" But instead of apologizing, they got angry too, and said they couldn't think of anything while being thrown against their seats, or that they couldn't reach me because they were belted into their seats. It was clear God had saved me by a miracle, so they congratulated me with slaps on the back.

I realized that there was no one I could rely on in an emergency, but only God could rescue me from death. Later, we discovered that the US helicopter pilots had swooped and done U-turns on purpose to frighten us Korean soldiers. I almost died because of that prank. Realizing that made me want to jump into the cockpit and throw the pilot out.

Even after that, we still had to do the helicopter training. I was so tense I could barely even move, so I decided to go last. Actually everyone wanted to go last because we were all rigid with fear, but whether first or last, it was all just as dangerous and just as terrifying. After everyone else had finished, my heart and my hands stiff with fear, I went out.

I held that rope ladder with a death grip, hunched my shoulders and climbed down, step by agonizing step. As the helicopter flew through the air, the ladder swayed back and forth as if it were blowing in a typhoon. I felt dizzy and everything started to fade to black, so I called God and screwed my eyes shut, then opened them again and struggled fiercely to complete the exercise.

Finally, we were all back on the ground. I lay down under the scorching sun, stretched my legs out, and didn't move until the next group had finished their training too.

'Good grief, today I almost died completing the training that's supposed to keep us alive under enemy attack. How can I possibly survive this? Who grabbed hold of me? Who saved me?' I thought.

That was the day
when death in the sky swallowed me
but spat me out.
God, who loves me,
granted me the grace of life
in the presence of death
To repay this grace,
until the end of my time on earth

I will always
live each day
as His body
loving only God and the Lord
with faithfulness and unwavering devotion

How did I avoid falling to my death when I was thrown toward the open door of the helicopter? The door rail was as thin as a ballpoint pen, yet the heel of my combat boot caught it, and I didn't fall. I could not have managed such an extraordinary thing if I had practiced it 100 times. Even if the heel on my boot had been a little more worn, I would have fallen to my death. I weighed 65 kg and my pack was 25 kg, so there was at least 90 kg (200 lbs) of weight flying toward the door. Even if someone had grabbed me, they would not have been able to stop me falling but would only have fallen with me.

One soldier thought I actually had fallen out. If I hadn't told them to fasten their seatbelts or if one of them hadn't done it, he would have fallen out of his seat and crashed into me as I was balancing miraculously on the rail, and we both would have fallen.

A premonition had compelled me to tell them to fasten their seatbelts, and through that, all our lives were saved. My concern for their lives ended up saving my own life as well.

I had a profound realization that I should live not only for myself but for my brothers and my neighbors also. God had protected me and let me survive when I valued the lives of my fellow soldiers as my own. I realized why Jesus said, "Love your neighbor as yourself." This command is for everyone.

Most people just care about their own safety, and yet, all human lives are connected and interwoven. If 11 players on a soccer team play well but just one of them accidentally knocks the ball into his own goal, the whole team loses. In the same way, every person living on the earth shares the same fate, such that we suffer if we fail to live for one another. In a community, one person's mistakes can harm everyone, and conversely, one person's success can benefit everyone. This is the law of the Creator, and it will endure as long as people live on the earth.

I am alive today because I survived that training exercise. That was the day death swallowed me, and only the Almighty saved me from its clutches.

SAFETY ISSUES AND ACCIDENTS

There are so many accidents that happen because people don't think through things properly, and people also lose their lives because they yield to others and somehow sacrifice themselves in the process. Most accidents are caused by unsafe behavior.

Accidents usually arise from carelessness. There was one delivery man who fell down a long staircase because the customer asked him to hurry, and he ended up dying. Another man fell off a cliff to his death while taking a photo for a newlywed couple because he took one too many steps backwards. Someone else was peeing behind a car when it reversed and hit him, killing him. On a rainy night, someone fell into a manhole and died.

Someone else was eating too fast and died from choking. People die from a concussion after slipping on a wet bathroom floor. People die from not fastening their seat belts. People die falling out of trees . People die from taking a wrong step high up on a construction site. People die from blood vessels bursting because they're in a fury. People die in car accidents by driving through red lights or stop signs because they're in a hurry. Many people also die from medical malpractice. In Korea alone, around 5,000 people are killed in traffic accidents every year. More than 17,000 people die from driving under the influence of alcohol, from illness, or from suicide. It's so regrettable when people die before their time because of failing to take proper care of their personal health and safety.

Sadly, too many people die before their life expectancy because they do not take sufficient care, are not properly alert, and don't invest in managing their health. Being extremely careful is like life's medicine, and it is wisdom that can save a life. The Bible tells us to take care of our lives.

During the war, many soldiers died bravely fighting the enemy, but many died simply because of accidents. Some soldiers had the misfortune to die on an operation because they lost their footing and rolled down the side of a mountain. Some soldiers returned safely from one operation and were preparing for the next: the first soldier asked the second to look into the gun barrel and see how well polished it was. Looking down the barrel, the second soldier said, "It will fire well – pull the trigger and see how smooth it is." Not knowing the gun was loaded, the first soldier pulled the trigger, and the second soldier was killed instantly, shot through the eye. He didn't die on the battlefield, but he died because of a safety breach.

Another soldier was awarded a few days off after doing well on an operation, so he went to play around at a brothel. He was beaten naked and killed by enemy soldiers. Another soldier was killed by a gun when he was climbing up a rocky slope. He was helping the soldier behind him, and as he pulled the other's gun to help him up, the man accidently touched the trigger and shot him dead. In another accident, some people were killed by an explosion at a garbage incinerator while watching the garbage burn.

One soldier survived many close calls with death over the course of one year fighting in Vietnam, but on the ship home, he fell off his bunk seven stories up because of his poor sleeping habits, landed on his head, and died of a concussion. There were also cases where soldiers mistook each other for enemies in the jungle and ended up fighting and killing each other. These were all accidents.

Even during an operation, if soldiers died trying to shoot the enemy without taking enough care of their own lives, that could be an accident too.

Those who died in the army during the war are treated as warriors and heroes, but it is somewhat shocking to know that many died because they failed to pay attention to what their superior officer said. Doing things perfectly is the only way to be perfectly safe from accidents.

Human beings live in ignorance, not knowing even five minutes, one minute, or ten seconds before their death. Why did the Creator make us with no knowledge of the future? No matter how much I think about it, that cannot be the case. I realized that people live in ignorance because they do not live as one with the Creator: so they know nothing of an impending accident, and they act unwisely and die. Ignorance kills people in the midst of daily life, not just on the battlefield.

The memory of nearly dying during helicopter training was so horrific I didn't even want to think about it while writing this book. Yet, when I took care of my neighbor's life as my own, God protected my life too. Through that, I gained my life that cannot be traded for the whole earth, and I write this book for everyone who yet lives and breathes.

If people pay a little more attention, even fatal accidents can be averted. Even those who are destined for death can escape it by riding on heaven's fortune. I cannot help but confess that the one who saved my life by His power is the Almighty.

God Almighty, who holds the earth suspended and spins it like a fan: the power is His, He can hold a man by one strand of hair and shake him this way and that, yet he will not fall. I realized that He displayed astounding power in saving me that day in the helicopter. I believe in His power, and with that faith, I live boldly as His hands and feet in this harsh world even today.

Yes, I exist
because I'm alive.

I deemed my brothers life,
my neighbors' life,
as my own
and God took care of my life;

He alone can do it,
can be responsible for my life.

I live amongst the signs
of the power of the Almighty.
I live because
I love and believe in Him alone.
I do His work
as His hands and feet.

I live for the purpose of
Him who created me,
therefore my purpose is also
being fulfilled.

Yes! I am happy
I am satisfied.

Whenever life brings difficulties, I struggle and pray. Then I remember this story, like the faint touches of inspiration, and I hear a voice say, "As then, so even now, I love you and I am with you, so do not worry but go forward boldly."

If I had fallen from the helicopter that day, how fast I would have plummeted! A person falling from the sky usually hits the ground head-first. There would have been no hope for me: my neck would certainly have broken, my head split open like a watermelon and my body shattered like an egg shatters against a rock.

Today as I write this book, I offer my thanksgiving once again to my guardian, the Almighty Trinity. Although everyone in the world has a different story, they were all rescued from death as I was. Their lives were saved, but many do not know because they hold different beliefs.

SPECIAL LECTURE AT THE NATIONAL TAIWAN UNIVERSITY

I gave a special lecture at the National Taiwan University auditorium in June of 1999. Twelve retired generals and 300 other people came to listen, as I lectured about life and death and told the story of my close call during helicopter training.

1999: THE AUTHOR LECTURING AT THE NATIONAL TAIWAN UNIVERSITY

I explained what happened using a model helicopter so everyone could understand, and they were all impressed by the miracle God had performed to save me.

One of the retired generals sitting up the front asked for the microphone because he wanted to share the story of his near-death experience. I handed the microphone to him and he told this story.

During the war, there was one time the soldiers were suddenly put on emergency alert. All the soldiers hid in foxholes (fighting holes) and the general was going to check on them, when one of the soldiers suddenly

| 1999: The author lecturing at the
national Taiwan University |

rushed out. The general shouted but the man ignored his superior officer and ran off. The general was angry and embarrassed, so he chased the soldier into another foxhole and shouted, "Why did you run off?" But the soldier just stared at him. Right then, a shell exploded in the previous foxhole, and it felt like the entire earth was shaken. Later they saw that the shell had exploded right where that soldier had been. so both the soldier and the general had been saved.

Everyone who heard that story gave a standing ovation. That battle was between China and Taiwan when their relationship was not good. The retired general asked me, "Wasn't it God who saved me from death?" And I replied that it was. He was deeply moved by God's love toward him. The rest of the audience were also moved and thankful. The other retired generals wanted to tell their stories too, but there was not enough time so I could not pass the microphone to all of them.

God has saved every single person from near-death situations, but they're not thankful because they don't know. I'm writing this book right now because when I'm older and I no longer have a clear voice to share this testimony, people can realize and give thanks by reading these stories. Although my life and circumstances are different from yours, you and I and everyone in the world can be reminded that our lives were spared because God helped us in the midst of danger.

Coming back to my story, I went deep into the mountains and prayed and spent years to understand my life and what had happened to me. I realized that the one who saved my life was the God who created me, and I asked Him how I could repay that grace. He told me to share this story so that everyone would know and give glory to God who saved them, and He said He would continue to watch over my life in return.

As I travel around the world, I share these stories and the gospel with both individuals and large crowds. I tell the stories of surviving more than 60 near-death experiences as each story comes to mind. Through that, I have seen so many people come to the thrilling understanding of how God saved their own lives.

People face death in different ways, but if you clearly realize that God Almighty saved you from death using creation, or people, or through His power within you, then you will overflow with abundant joy.

There is a saying that each person faces death three times in their life, but I disagree. I think it's more than that. I, myself, narrowly escaped death more than 60 times, 30 on the battlefield and 30 while living in this tough world. And these are just the cases that I know about: there would be many more if I could count everything God did to protect my life. I cannot help but be thankful for that. God saved me and used me as His hands and feet to help people from many nations believe in and love Him, so that both their bodies and spirits would be saved.

People know only what is within their understanding: they know nothing of what God does in secret. Realizing how God saved them from near-death situations is realizing deep things about God. The only way for God to help you again is for you to offer thanks and gratitude to Him. God desires to give more to those who are thankful and to give love to those who love Him.

THE DAY I CUT MY FINGERNAILS, TOENAILS, AND HAIR AND PUT THEM IN A WHITE ENVELOPE

In early 1967, after acclimatizing to the tropics and completing our emergency training in the Nha Trang area, our company moved to the foothills of Tuy Hoa Honba, where the North Vietnamese troops and the Vietcong were waiting.

We dug trenches and set up a stronghold in the village of Furong on the road near Honba Mountain. The area was low-lying and became waterlogged easily, which was a real problem in the rainy season when we had to drain the water.

We engaged in many ambush operations and night search operations, some big and some small. Whenever we left camp, we had to pass through the putrid, stinking water. Many bison got shot during the war, and their rotting corpses floated in the water alongside the corpses of enemy soldiers. Whenever we had to wade through the stagnant water that came up to our waists, germs contaminated our whole bodies, so we were itchy and smelled hideous. We all vomited, passing through that disgusting water.

Even though it was more than 45 years ago, I remember as clear as day. Just thinking about it brings back the rotten stench, the sight of maggots and the urge to vomit. I'm afraid of what I will see in my dreams tonight. How shocking that odor was! All the soldiers in the rifle corps suffered terribly from that stench during search operations.

Oh, the war

The stench it gives off

124

The stench of rotting life
Oh, the soldiers
The stench they give off
The stench of hunting life
Oh, the one who values life
The fragrance they would give off
The fragrance of peace
Surely
Flowers will bloom and bear fruit
And the kingdom of peace
Will come

Honba Mountain was a key position for the entire region of Tuy Hoa where the local Vietcong and North Vietnamese regular forces were hiding out. They were the enemies facing the White Horse 28th Regiment. In order to prevent them attacking and infiltrating Tuy Hoa City, the 3rd Company (the QRF) was deployed at the base of the mountain.

I was assigned an M79 grenade launcher as a shooter in the White Horse Unit, 9th Division, 28th Regiment, 1st Battalion, 3rd Company, 1st Platoon, 2nd Squad. A squad included nine people, and there were four squads in a platoon, which had 41 people including five from platoon HQ: a platoon leader, a fugleman, a senior sergeant, a messenger or platoon leader radio man, and a medic.

One day we received a directive from above: for soldiers who died in battle, only their cremated ashes would be repatriated home, and not the corpse. We had to trim our nails and toenails and put them in an envelope to be kept with the unit. So our squad sat together in the barracks and were cutting off hair and nails to put in envelopes.

People are usually more afraid of death than anything else, and for us too, we couldn't help but to be haunted by the fear of death. We had travelled to the battlefield leaving loved ones behind – wives, children, parents, brothers, girlfriends – and we had arrived at a crossroads between life and death. In case we died in battle, we were trimming our hair and nails so they could be sent back home along with our ashes. We were brave enough when facing our enemies, but the anxiety and fear at other times made it hard to stop weak thoughts. Just like a bonfire burns down to ashes and then dies out, a life in the war could end up as only a handful of ashes, and then disappear completely.

I didn't feel quite as anxious as the others because I had my faith in God and Jesus. To help the suffering of their hearts disappear, I told my fellow soldiers to pray for a safe return home, since God was in control of our lives and not the enemy. They replied, "We are not Christians, so even if we pray, God won't answer. You're a believer, so why don't you pray for us?"

We looked each other in the eyes and exchanged firm but heartbreaking words, expressing our determination to return home safely. One soldier, Lee Tae-Seong, said he must surely return alive since he was engaged and was the only son of three generations. I demanded, "I don't have a girlfriend or a wife or children, so does that mean I need to be killed?" The others laughed. "Corporal Jeong always prays for us, so he mustn't die."

| We sat around in the barracks and cut our fingernails, toenails, and hair |

We all sealed our envelopes, wrote our unit details, and sent them off to regiment HQ via platoon HQ. Our squad leader seemed to be feeling a lot of mixed emotions, and was acting kind of anxious after sending the envelopes, so he ordered Sergeant Kim, "Go buy me two cans of beer." Sergeant Kim ran there and back like lightning to bring the beer, and the squad leader gulped down both cans without any side snacks, as usual. The soldiers nodded to each other as a signal to lighten the mood. "How can you enjoy beer so much without any snacks?" We asked him, while he drank by himself.

The squad leader chuckled, "People who hold their drink well don't need beer snacks. Just the beer by itself is delicious, why would I eat snacks?" He looked around at us, "Hey, what are you afraid of? While you're alive, drink, have fun – do whatever you want to your heart's content. Live fast and die young." Everyone smiled or laughed back, agreeing with each other that he seemed to be living a fun life in his own way.

Sergeant Yoo was a bit of a sycophant and second to none when it came to drinking. He quickly brought in dried squid snacks and C-ration to the squad leader. In that environment, people had to be very clever to avoid punishment and get hit less.

Sergeant Yoo was always tactfully saying the right things and he behaved in an obsequious manner when he noticed the squad leader was preparing to blow up at us. The squad leader grinned at Yoo, "You love to drink. Since we're all feeling down today, why don't you bring out a bottle of soju?" Yoo, who loved soju, pulled out a bottle he had hidden in his pack. As he was taking a large swig, he looked at me with embarrassment in his eyes and said, "Please understand." We were quite close, and he had told me a few times that he would stop drinking.

Our squad leader, though, drank far too much. Sometimes he set a flame to his drinking bowl and we saw it ignited immediately, fire shooting up. I was shocked, wondering how he could put away hard liquor like that. "Is your stomach iron-plated?" I asked, with a smile.

He looked back at me and said, "Try it, it tastes great. You can't understand me and we don't see eye to eye because you don't drink."

"Bad things often happen because you drink too much and don't understand me and our squad members." I spoke indirectly, hoping he would realize.

He replied with a smile, "Here, eat the squid then, since you can't drink." He tossed a sparing amount of that expensive snack to me, and when the soldiers next to me clamored for it too, he threw us the rest. Tearing the squid apart, we offered the squid fins back to the squad leader, who grinned and ordered Sergeant Yoo, "Hey! Bring some more cans of beer. At least let the squad have a drink. And you, fool, if you're thirsty, drink. You're a man, you should be able to drink a glass of Johnnie Walker or something. Do you know why I was mad? You can't drink so you can't be my drink buddy." He sighed.

I asked, "What concentration is that alcohol you're drinking?"
"This? It's over 90% alcohol." He answered.
Soju (Korean distilled spirits) is 25% alcohol, so what he was drinking was almost four times stronger, so I asked how he could drink such strong liquor. He said he mixed a little water into it, and kept drinking, saying he didn't even mind if it killed him.

People know that alcohol is bad for them, but they can't quit because they got used to it. Too many people die before their time because of alcohol. After I was discharged, I looked for my old squad leader at a Vietnam War Veterans' reunion, but I couldn't find him. I believe he passed away before he even reached the age of 50.

The smell of alcohol makes me want to vomit. As my squad leader and Sergeant Yoo next to me drank, that smell made my nose wrinkle in disgust and numbed my senses for a long time after. I couldn't tell those seniors to stop drinking, and I couldn't build my own barrack and sleep by myself, either. When they and my other squad members drank a lot and got buzzed, that tiny barrack smelled like a brewery. I hated the smell so much that I used to even go outside and face the mosquitos, preferring to work over putting up with the smell.

Considering how I couldn't stand the stench of alcohol, my future living in the barracks looked gloomy at first, but as time passed, I adjusted and could no longer distinguish the smell of liquor from the smell of putrid water. Many people think alcohol has health benefits, and drinking makes them feel good, however, alcohol causes a lot more harm than good. People make so many mistakes when they drink.

Alcohol is fermented food. Seven hours after we eat, the food ferments naturally inside us, similar to moderate drinking. There's really no need to drink alcohol. Even rice, for example, naturally ferments internally and gives you the same pleasant feeling as drinking, but it's good for your health and doesn't lead to any of the poor decisions associated with alcohol. Even non-drinkers 'drink' in this way through the food they consume.

In this way, the Creator made a natural way for people to enjoy food, but people just live their lives without realizing it. And some people go further, creating stronger and more stimulating alcohol, which makes them feel good in the moment but harms their health in the long run, and even leads to death.

It's not just alcohol. Taking drugs or stimulants to feel love and excitement other than in the natural way that the Creator intended are all examples of crossing the line. Despite the temporary high people gain, anything that goes beyond the natural law will ultimately make people grow sick and even die.

FIGHTING, WORRIES, AND ANXIETY STEM FROM IGNORANCE

People cannot get off the wheel of life unless they can escape the environment or situation that entraps them. Those who are ignorant live without meaning and fight for no purpose.

North and South Vietnam were neighbors, geographically: culturally and linguistically they were one family, one bloodline. However, they fought and grew distant, and ideologies and customs changed. Eventually, the conflict grew to the point where the whole world was involved in efforts to stop the fight.

It was strange to consider those I had never seen before as my enemy, and it seemed absurd to wage war against them and shoot men I had never argued with, without exchanging a word. I was told to shoot them on sight, and to risk my life fighting them because they were the enemy, but I couldn't help thinking, 'Why should I fight them like this?'

The United States was responsible for South Vietnam, so they had a reason to fight the North Vietnamese troops, but for us, there was no good reason to go around fighting against the young Vietnamese people. Our true fight was to peacefully separate the warring sides, to help and comfort civilians, to teach them what they needed to know and to do what we could to protect the cause of freedom.

Anyway, war is complicated, troublesome, and embarrassing. If we hate and fight, there is no end to the fighting, whether for individuals or nations. It only causes loss for everyone in the end.

Only the omniscient and omnipotent God could stop the hostilities. Compared to the past, human ideology and the way the world lives have changed so much. People fall in love and make families, lives are interwoven by trade, art, and tourism – this ideal world of peace is like a dream come true. If we fought each other to the end, everyone would die, so the Creator stepped in to end the war and make the world of peace we see today.

In my view, it's everyone's duty to live at peace, loving others and letting go of the bitterness and resentment caused by war, fighting, and death. The peace and harmony of the present are the only way to make an ideal world.

The city of Tuy Hoa in Vietnam, where the White Horse 9th Division, 28th Regiment, Goblin Unit was stationed half a century ago, is now a beautiful tropical city, having left its past far behind. That place where nations battled has become a destination even for veterans of the war to visit and enjoy the food and culture, while swapping old stories and laughing aloud, like a dream come true.

When we were stationed in the village of Furong in Tuy Hoa, in squad barracks constructed from C-ration crates, the members of my squad feared for the future while packaging up our nail and hair samples to send them to our homeland along with our ashes in case we were killed in a battle. In the end, we passed through that valley of death with God's protection, and came out alive despite numerous search and ambush operations and major battles. If we had known we would survive everything, we would not have had that anxiety, but we all lived under the fear of death and endless worries because it was thought that around 70 percent of soldiers would die.

There is no need to worry and be anxious about the future: it only steals a person's health and confidence. The best option is to rely only on God, not lose heart, and to be thankful and joyful even in the face of death. I believe it is God's will for man to live without knowing the future, yet God also shares secrets about what is to come with those who love Him. If people love and trust Him, He does not let them worry unnecessarily. He repays each person according to their deeds.

I HEARD A VOICE IN MY HEART: "YOU WILL SURELY NOT DIE BUT RETURN HOME ALIVE."

This was about a month after arriving in Vietnam, when we were staying in Nha Trang. Every day, fellow soldiers saved the instant coffee from their C-ration to take home. They had big hopes of buying TVs or cassette recorders with the generous pay we received monthly. For me, I thought that even if I couldn't take anything home with me, my life would be the greatest gift.

Our unit was replacing a Marine Corps unit. I asked a Marine, "How long have you been in Vietnam?"

"Almost a year," he answered.

"What's the war really like? How many have died, from the nine in your squad?"

"Six dead and three survivors," he answered. "Not a bad outcome, so far." On hearing that, the fear of death struck me anew and I was terrified. 'How can two-thirds of the soldiers die?' I thought.

In shock I wondered if I could possibly return home safely. I turned back to him and asked when he was due to finish his tour. He was almost in tears as he answered, "This is my final month of duty, but there is no guarantee I will live."

I asked him if he believed in God and Jesus, and he said he didn't, so I offered a deal: "If I pray for you and you go home safely, you have to believe in God!"

He laughed, "Are you sure?"

I looked him dead in the eye: "I guarantee you, absolutely."

"I will surely believe in Him!" he answered.

After hearing this soldier telling me that two-thirds of the soldiers could die, I was shocked and realized that I shouldn't worry about anything else except my life. So I lifted my head and prayed, gazing up at the blue sky. "God, I see that it would be a miracle for me to return home safely from this battlefield. Please, save my life. It seems clear that I might die while fighting in a battle. If I live, I believe that only you, God, will have saved me, and I will use my life only as you want, until I die. As Jesus says in the Bible, 'What good is it for a man to gain the whole world, yet forfeit his soul?' Here in the face of death, I realized the value of my life.

"Life is so precious: it cannot be traded for the entire world. Therefore, if you save me, I will live a joyful and valuable life as if I had been granted the whole earth. I will not kill the enemy, but treat them with your love. In return, let them not kill me," I petitioned earnestly. I clung to God and Jesus and promised that if I lived, I would pray for the lives of those who did not believe.

At that moment, hot tears streamed down my face. The blue sky seemed even clearer and bluer, as if it were the eye of God, and I felt in a fiery way that God was listening to my prayer. A quiet voice spoke in my heart: "You will return home safely."

I was so moved that tears welled up again. I was so relieved and happy. "Thank you! When I return home, I will preach the gospel and evangelize people for the rest of my life. God, Jesus, you will see it."

Just as God promised, I returned home safely despite many brushes with death. I suffered greatly through hundreds of military operations and battles, and was almost killed 30 times when chased and shot at by the enemy. Nevertheless, I escaped all of that and went home safely. I went home with not only my life, but a TV and a cassette recorder, which was very exciting for me at the time. I have a large Akai recorder similar to that one as a souvenir that brings back those days that are long gone.

Veterans from the war gather at reunions or other events to talk about our time in Vietnam, even though it was more than 45 years ago. We remind each other how great a miracle it is for us to meet, after returning alive. Some of us are believers and some not, but we all agree that only God could have saved us and brought us home.

We suffered to the point of death, and yet we lived. Back then, there was not a single day we didn't feel the fear of death and the anxieties of war. All those worries were unnecessary. Worrying excessively about the future only torments a person's heart: there is no need to worry.

SOLDIERS MOVING THROUGH TOWN TO THE FIELD OF OPERATION

IN THE VIETNAM

THE CONFESSION OF A VIETCONG SOLDIER WHO SURRENDERED

WAR 1966-1969

"God, the ruler of human life, is more likely to protect the life of a person of God: a person who recognizes and serves Him."

CHAPTER 5

THE CONFESSION OF A VIETCONG SOLDIER WHO SURRENDERED

THE DAY WE LOOKED FOR THE ENEMY IN THE CAVES OF HONBA MOUNTAIN AS ADVANCE GUARDS

The 3rd Company was a part of the QRF (Quick Reaction Force), so we were on standby for emergencies 24/7. We were always alert and on our toes: there was not a single day we could rest easy. In fact, being out on an operation would have been less stressful. There were many times we would arrive back at the base after an operation, and without even being able to remove our packs, we would get sent out on another emergency operation.

I felt very resentful towards our enemies. If we just sat around, then the enemy would invade and attack to take away our lives whenever the opportunity arose, but protecting our lives meant exhaustion and endless weariness, just trying to survive one battle after the next. Not only was there no time to complain or even get discouraged, but we were risking our lives in a foreign land with no way to return home until our tour of duty was over.

One day we were faced with a company-level emergency, so everyone in the company was brought in on the operation. Our destination was a rocky cliff on Honba Mountain, which was an utter nightmare to climb and would have drawn a sigh of despair even from a monkey. We had already carried out many operations on Honba Mountain. Everyone carried combat rations, 300 bullets, a tent, and a gun in our packs, while climbing that steep cliff. As we struggled up, we felt like our souls, called 'hon' in Korean, were being drained out of us. Prior to the deployment to Vietnam, we had already endured three months of excruciating special training and guerrilla tactics on Yongmun Mountain in Yangpyeong. We scaled the cliff like monkeys, swinging between branches as if they were ropes.

That day, we were told to undertake a search operation on the fourth ridge of Honba Mountain, after we were informed by civilians that more than 20 enemy soldiers were stationed in caves there. We tightened our belt of alertness and departed to the area of operation on foot, fully armed, at 2pm.

Sergeant Yoo and I were assigned as advance guards, which was a task that would strike any heart with terror and the fear of death. The advance guard was sent 20-50 meters ahead of the main body of soldiers, to conceal their movement from the waiting enemy, and to find the enemy before they found us, by checking for any kind of movement. After that, we were to notify our troops following the 5W and 1H rule (what, where, when, who, why, how).

The advance guards were the first to be spotted by the enemy and the first to be engaged, so they were often killed. They had to stay out in front to protect the rest of the troops, so they were also first in line to die from booby traps, landmines, or improvised explosive devices, or to walk into wire fences or pits dug by the enemy.

Those pits were usually embedded with sharp bamboo spears, and sometimes were even filled with poisonous snakes, so anyone who fell in would be stabbed by the spears and bitten by the snakes. The spears were smeared with cow dung so that they would infect you with tetanus, making those 2-meter deep pits into the worst kind of death-traps. They were so well concealed that they were impossible to see, day or night. We could do nothing except sharpen our senses and embrace the fear of death as our best protection.

Enemy soldiers would also hide out in the jungle or between rocks and follow our movements with binoculars, so they always saw us, no matter how quietly we moved or what size group we were with. Because of all this, the advance guard was on such extreme alert that our eyes would become bloodshot with the strain. The advance guard could be considered the sacrificial lamb: seen and killed first to protect those behind. Another way to look at it was to say they had the most important mission, determining the fate of the whole troop. The advance guard was like the radar, and had to be in top condition at all times.

I served two tours in Vietnam, spanning three years of battles and more than 70 assignments as advance guard. Every single day on the battlefield was filled with the fear of death, but advance guard duty was even worse -- like walking on a tightrope of death. The advance guard carried the greatest risk, and were the most likely to die. The enemy would hide in the jungle until they saw us, then shoot us in the head or chest at close range and run off immediately. It is extremely difficult to catch the one who shoots first, so seeing first and shooting first usually meant survival.

Each group usually had two soldiers in the advance guard. On jungle missions, one person had to slash a path through the undergrowth with a machete while the other went ahead, gun at the ready, to watch for any sign of movement and warn those behind. Because of the difficulties involved, advanced guard duty was sometimes done on rotation. Slashing away at trees and weeds with a machete is noisy: it makes a noise even if you try to do it holding your breath and moving like a ghost, so the enemy would hear, from hiding, and fire on that person. However, without cutting through the thorns and bushes, it was impossible to pass through, so there was no choice but to do it as quietly as possible. That's why I said we were moving forward while paying attention in every direction until our eyes were bloodshot.

That day, Sergeant Yoo and I struggled through the jungle for about two and a half hours, using 2 foot long machetes to cut through the weeds and thorns. My whole body was drenched with sweat. The company followed 50 meters behind us and with a gap of 5 meters between each person, but having those numbers behind us didn't give peace of mind. The enemy could be watching through binoculars, and they could attack with grenade launchers and blow us to pieces from 200 or 300 meters away, or they could spring out in front, shoot the advance guard, and disappear into the forest. The safest tactic was just to move as silently as possible and avoid being detected. Sometimes the Vietcong let the advance guard pass first and attacked the main unit in order to inflict higher casualties. That's why, once an operation began, all the soldiers would hunker down like shrimp, glancing in all directions and moving stealthily.

We were guaranteed the enemy would be at the destination that day, so as we slashed our way through the jungle, the thought of the enemy watching us terrified me and my whole body was tensed up and dripping sweat. Every time we walked that dark valley of death, my only way to get through it was to put my faith in the one and only God Almighty, my savior, and to push away my fear. Still, those operations where we had to flush the enemy out of the mountain caves where they were hiding made my legs tremble and my hair stand on end.

IN THE VIETNAM WAR 1966-1969

The tropical forest was full of tough thorn bushes and weeds. After the advance guard passed through that impenetrable tangle as silently as possible, and when it was safe, we would signal those behind to follow. The main body of soldiers would wait for us, squatting in the undergrowth and watching every direction while the path was being made, which was pretty hard on them, too, with the sun beating down on them relentlessly and the overgrown weeds radiating suffocating hot air. It was as miserable as a dead-end alley in the concrete jungle of life.

Paying close attention to whether the birds were chirping louder than usual or to any breaking twig that might mean enemy movement, Sergeant Yoo and I quietly cut our way through the jungle for an hour. I knew for a fact that no one had ever passed that way before. The birds spread their wings and flapped off in surprise when they saw us, which made me feel less tense. Yoo said we should only cut the thick thorn bushes and clear enough room for our bodies to pass through, and not bother clearing the path completely. After about two hours had passed, we came out of the jungle on the other side. Instead of the jungle, we now saw large trees, close together, and rocks the size of small huts stacked up in random mounds. When we reached a grove of trees, the sweat dripped off our clothes as if we'd been caught in heavy rain, and the stifling heat, 38°C or 40°C (100°F~104°F), made it hard to breathe.

Pausing to sit and watch for any movement, I was nagged by an incessant feeling that something was wrong. We both poked each other, and asked if the other could feel it – that fear, the sense of foreboding that made our hair stand on end even though we were wearing helmets. Yoo felt it too. We were both extremely tense. It felt like the enemy was right behind a rock or tree and would shoot us at any second.

| CHAPTER 5 - THE CONFESSION OF A VIETCONG SOLDIER WHO SURRENDERED | 145

Crouching down, we moved backwards as quickly as possible, holding our breath, our eyes darting in every direction. We could see no one, and yet, our hair stood up, goosebumps covered our skin, our hearts pounded and all we could feel was that all-encompassing fear that the enemy would find and shoot us in an instant. We both decided that the feeling meant for sure the enemy was nearby, so we backed up another 5 or 6 meters.

After a brief moment of prayer, I felt by inspiration that the enemy was right in front of us. The revelation was from God Almighty who has always kept me safe, and He enlightened me by letting me feel it. Yoo and I squatted behind a tree. I whispered, "There are Vietcongs watching us from somewhere close by, or at least, this is definitely somewhere they come." I said that we should not move, but wait and see, and I notified the platoon leader too. A few minutes later, an announcement came through on the walkie talkie that we had reached the exact location where the civilians had said the cave was. As the advance guard, we were told to stand aside and take a break, while keeping an eye out.

I thought to myself, 'Of course! This is why I was suddenly afraid and my hair was standing up so hard it could've lifted my helmet: we arrived at the enemy's camp. I could sense it.'

People sometimes feel things intuitively or get sudden inspirations. God, our Creator, gave us a kind of spiritual radar, better than anything modern technology can offer, that can detect life-threatening dangers and help us avoid them. Spiritual inspirations and intuitions are not limited by distance, and can sense things thousands of miles away. Spiritual people can clearly see the future through spiritual inspiration and power. If we communicate with God, He enlightens us and speaks to us through nature and revelations.

Since our advance guard duty was finished, the platoon leader sent us down away from the area where the cave was, and the company forces set off on the search operation. The Vietnamese civilian informants and the military translator spoke through the loudhailer, telling those in the cave to surrender and gain their freedom, since they were surrounded, and that they would not be killed if they surrendered and came out. After 20 minutes of this, there was still no response, but the informants said it was definitely the place. The Vietnamese informants with us had been active in the Vietcong forces but, unable to bear the misery, had escaped to seek freedom, and had surrendered to the Korean Army. They had revealed the location of their former comrades so that they too could surrender and obtain freedom.

A NEAR-DEATH EXPERIENCE WHILE BATHING

While our company was carrying out the mission, Yoo and I had been relieved of duty as the advance guard and we walked 40 meters back down the mountain, away from the cave. We heard cool, running water between the rocks, so we followed the sound because we were drenched with sweat and very thirsty. We finally found a spring and a pool of water two meters in diameter, knee deep and clean. It was a very pleasant surprise, to find that clean, cool water up on the mountain, deep enough to wash in. After hours of tension and hacking our way through weeds and thorns in the jungle, we really wanted to jump in fully clothed, but we were still on operation, so we decided to have a bit more of a look around.

Above us, we could hear the army translator shouting in Vietnamese over the loudhailer, telling the enemy they had nowhere to go and should surrender. Judging from the lack of gunfire, I thought perhaps our efforts had been in vain and nothing was going to happen. It seemed as if the Vietcong had somehow detected our approach and scattered like wild rabbits – if they had been in the cave, something would have happened by now, so Yoo and I felt less anxious.

I wondered, 'How did this spring come to be here in the mountains? Is this a natural pool?'

Seeing that flowing water, we stuck our faces in and drank like cows. The water was so good and refreshing, cooling us from the inside. We rolled up our sleeves and dipped our arms in the cool water, feeling our temperature fall and our energy return. Since we had finished our advance guard duty, we desperately wanted to remove our clothes, drenched in fear and sweat, and have a wash. Impulsively, we decided to leave our guns near the spring, wash at lightning speed, and get back out.

Throwing off our filthy clothes, we jumped in the cold water. We washed each other's backs, scrubbing off all the sweat and grime, and washed our hair, feeling revitalized. The water was icy, probably flowing from deep under the mountain, so we cooled down completely. We jumped into that cold water because of the stress of the hours we had just spent as advance guard, and since we stumbled upon such a nice pool where we could drink and wash. I sincerely thanked God for creating nature.

In terms of faith, my philosophy was always to be thankful to God, because when we're not thankful, complaints come out instead. Nothing good goes to those who complain against Heaven. God gives us laughter when we give Him something to laugh about, and gives us frowns when we frown at Him. Dunking my sweaty head in the cool water seemed to clear my mind, and when Yoo next to me dunked his head under as well, he also seemed to come to his senses because, "Thank you, God," just popped out of his mouth, and that definitely wasn't something he would normally say.

We cooled off in the water and were drinking out of our hands. All of a sudden, noises! We heard the sound of people among the big rocks that surrounded the pool. Who was it? We stared tensely at each other, not moving, but listening fearfully. We would have got a shock even if we had heard soldiers from our own company, because we were in the water, but the voices were whispering unintelligibly in Vietnamese. They were definitely Vietcong, so we both panicked and froze, but the whispering and footsteps continued, and we decided they were right behind the rocks surrounding the pool.

I grabbed Yoo and whispered in his ear: "They're Vietcong, Vietcong! They're passing by right behind that rock."
Yoo whispered back into my ear, "Vietcong! It's the Vietcong, what do we do?"

We were scared witless and gripped each other tightly. I sensed strongly that the Vietcong were watching us, and we nervously looked away in the hopes of avoiding eye contact.

If the Vietcong were watching us, they would be only 3-4 meters away — maybe that's why my mind was so blank, as if my head was as empty as space, and my wet hair seemed to stand on end in shock. My heart swelled with the fear of imminent death, and I was afraid right down to my soul. My body felt paralyzed, and I could feel the eyes of the Vietcong on us, and hear their whispers just behind.

| The terrifying moment when the Vietcong appeared behind the author and Sergeant Yoo as they were bathing, and aimed their guns |

Right then, I heard a gun being loaded. I tried to run even though I didn't have my clothes on but my body was rooted to the spot. We could do nothing but stand there shaking in fear, eyes popping out and looking in the other direction, stiff as corpses. Our guns and helmets were just 2-3 meters out of reach, but I knew if we tried to grab them, we would be shot. That thought alone was paralyzing. Next thing, I got a strong feeling that we were about to be shot in the back of the head. I desperately prayed to God to not get shot. We weren't even breathing, afraid that if we turned around or moved, they would shoot. There was nothing we could do.

I had no idea what to do and just kept calling God and Jesus in my heart. I was burning up with tension as I stood there in the water.

People tend to seek God at the point their life reaches a dead end. Facing my death in that moment, I also called God desperately, and Yoo did the same, both of us pleading for swift salvation from that deadly situation. Some people repent of their sins in the moments before death, but in that moment, repenting didn't cross my mind for a second, I could only feel my head spin. I was entirely too anxious to think. All I could hear was the enemy loading their rifles, and all my mind could see was their guns being pointed at us, ready to shoot. I prayed God would jam their guns. What we felt in that moment, what we saw and heard, expecting to hear gunshots and feel bullets fly in a second – who could understand it? In that situation, my parents could not save me, though they loved me, nor could my siblings or comrades do anything to help.

Right at that moment, Yoo hissed in my ear that we should go for our guns, but I grabbed his hand and stopped him, whispering that we'd be shot if we moved. I tried to analyze the situation from the enemy's point of view, at the same time whispering to Yoo and calling out to God, so my thoughts were a jumbled mess. I felt like a prisoner sentenced to capital punishment in front of the firing squad.

I begged and pleaded with all my heart. My dying wish, my plea, was to Him, God whom I trusted, to save me. But there was no answer, no feeling or inspiration, so I thought perhaps it was too late, and that surviving was no longer an option. I couldn't tell how much time had passed as we stood there, frozen in fear.

I urgently wanted to see who was behind us, but I strongly felt they would shoot the moment we turned our heads, so we stood there, like statues. Then, a tiny feeling came to me: I felt like God was standing next to me, protecting me, and I wasn't going to die. From that point, the fear began to leave me.

I heard more footsteps and whispering, and the sound of guns being cocked. "They're going to shoot us now," I panicked and lost my mind. My body felt paralyzed and I couldn't even move my neck, but moments later, the footsteps moved past us and slowly faded, until there was no more sound. All was quiet. The Vietcong had apparently left.

My paralyzed body began to loosen up. It felt like my soul had left my body and was only now returning. Still grasping each other, Yoo and I started to breathe. "We're alive. It seems like they left." We quickly got dressed, unlocked our guns and loaded them, then went to see what had happened.

We found a large crevice between two rocks, wide enough for a person to crawl and face toward the spring. I was sure that the Vietcong had been watching us through that gap. At the thought of them aiming their guns at us, I was covered in goosebumps and my head spun.

We searched, but no one was around.

I was confident the Vietcong had disappeared earlier when we heard the footsteps receding, so we finally lowered our guns and breathed a sigh of relief. All of the stress finally got to me, and I couldn't think straight. My body ached all over and my legs were shaking. Looking around, I saw a cave.

"Hey look, there's a cave over here."
Going closer, we found a cave entrance in a jumble of rocks and boulders, with a path leading from it. Inspecting the path, we could see many people had recently passed by. The Vietcong must have seen the Korean troops approaching the front of the cave, and fled out the back, through this opening 40 meters away, where they had seen us. Obviously, they had been using the spring for drinking and washing. The thing I couldn't figure out, though, was why they had just passed by us when we were defenseless.

At that moment, a call came through on the radio from above us: the platoon leader told everyone including the advance guards to regroup, as the operation was finished for the day. On our way up, we inspected the path behind the rock, which led between the back entrance of the cave and the spring. On seeing it, the situation became clear: the Vietcong were escaping out the back entrance of the cave when they saw us, but after debating whether to kill us or not, they decided to just run. I knew for sure because I had heard their guns being loaded just 3-4 meters behind us, and heard their whispers and footsteps.

Without thinking, I exclaimed, "God Almighty, the omniscient One, saved my life!" Even Yoo, who didn't believe in God, confessed that God saved him that day. Or rather, he said that God saved me and he survived because he was with me.

The sun was beginning to set. We heard the loudhailer again, telling everyone that the operation was over and the advance guards should also quickly evacuate and return to the unit, so we stopped talking and headed back to the others, thoughts swirling in our heads. We both agreed not to breathe a word of what had happened while we were bathing in the spring.

After returning to base and cleaning up, I thought back on the day's events. I shuddered at the memory. It almost seemed like it had been a dream. No one other than Yoo and myself could ever really understand what we had been through. Since we had no one else to confide in, the two of us talked for a long time that night. We should have died that day, naked and helpless, but instead we had escaped with our lives. I said we should thank God together.

We couldn't come up with any other theory except that the Vietcong had escaped out through the back of the cave near the spring while the rest of the team were searching. It's just that we hadn't noticed because we'd been bathing. The search team had said they hadn't been able to go too deep into the cave because it was just too dangerous, with boulders and passages shooting off in all directions, so in the end, they had come back out the way they went in.

Like ants crawling around in the gravel, the Vietcong moved around the cave through big piles of boulders and rocks. It would be easy to get lost in that kind of cave: if you went in too far, you might not be able to find the way out, or if you took a wrong exit you could end up somewhere completely different. Inexperienced cave searches were sometimes fatal.

| THE AUTHOR WITH SERGEANT YOO, CARRYING OUT THEIR DUTY AS ADVANCE
GUARD DURING THE SEARCH OPERATION |

THE MYSTERY SOLVED THROUGH THE VIETCONG CONFESSION: 'AH, THE HONBA MOUNTAIN'S ANGEL OF DEATH CAME TO CATCH ME!'

The other soldiers who went with us on that operation were really irritated about wasting the whole day hiking to hell and back because of a false tip-off. Of course, the information wasn't false – Sergeant Yoo and I knew all too well, but we couldn't say anything. We could easily have solved the mystery by telling them that the Vietcong fled through the back opening of the cave, but the dratted bath we took meant we had to keep our mouths shut. We only took a bath because we'd finished our duties and nothing much was happening, and of course because it was hot enough to make a person pass out. Still, taking a bath in the middle of an operation would get us in serious trouble, whatever the reason. There was no way to sound the alarm when the enemy were passing by, because they would have killed us, and even though we wanted to report it afterwards, it was too late.

After getting back, everyone kept saying how strange the whole operation had been. The information should have been accurate, we were able to find the cave, and we even found evidence that their base was located there. So people wondered if the Vietcong found out about our operation and fled, or if the informers had been misleading us. Most people blamed the civilian informers and accused them of providing false information. A guilty conscience needs no accuser: I could not say anything even though I knew, and my heart was gripped with the frustration of being unable to do anything.

Sergeant Yoo believed in the existence of a divine being but was not a church-goer. That evening, we were too restless to eat or sleep properly. When we did finally drift off out of exhaustion, we were suddenly awoken and told that the company commander was asking for the advance guards from that day's operation. The platoon leader had sent a soldier to bring us right away. Somewhat befuddled with sleep, I asked him again and he repeated that the company commander was looking for the advance guards from the Honba Mountain operation.

As we ran to the commander's office, we couldn't help wondering why we were being called out in the middle of the night. When an officer calls his subordinates, it's almost never for compliments but only for rebukes. We got more and more anxious, so we ran faster. The commander, instead of being asleep, was urgently asking for us in the middle of the night – it was certain that no small event was behind this. My heart was pounding with anxiety and I couldn't get the thought of our clandestine bath out of my head.

The command center for Company Commander Chan-Ki Min was down in the basement bunker, a medium size room of about 16 square meters (178 ft2). I had never been inside before. We found it brightly lit, with two unfamiliar Vietnamese standing inside. They looked like Vietcong. We stood before the commander, and Sergeant Yoo, who was senior to me, reported.
"Commander, Sergeant Geun-Tae Yoo plus one reporting as ordered."
"At ease," he replied. "Were you two the advance guard today during the Honba Mountain search operation?"

"Yes, sir. That is correct."
"Did you guys take a bath in the mountain?"

Yoo and I were startled – how could he possibly know about the bath? We just stood there flustered, trying to figure out what to say. Unexpectedly, the commander smiled and told us to relax and just tell him what happened, since the two Vietcongs had come down the mountain today and turned themselves in and told him everything. Seeing the commander smile helped us loosen up a little. Wanting to verify the report from the Vietcong, the commander asked us to report what we had seen and heard during the Honba Mountain operation. He told us that while the two men were dressed like civilians, they were Vietcong soldiers who had been living in the cave we had searched that afternoon, and had come to surrender. They had been with 14 other Vietcong soldiers when our company had set up speakers at the cave telling them to surrender, and while fleeing out the back entrance 50 meters away, they had seen two naked Korean soldiers taking a bath. The commander asked if that had been us.

| HONBA MOUNTAIN |

| AFTER LISTENING TO THE TWO VIETCONG WHO TURNED THEMSELVES IN, THE
COMPANY COMMANDER CALLED THOSE WHO WERE ON ADVANCE GUARD DUTY
DURING THE SEARCH OPERATION AND ASKED ABOUT THE BATHING INCIDENT |

We could not deny it any longer, so we confessed everything. We told him that after our long and arduous stint as advance guard, we were dripping sweat and almost passing out from the heat, and since our duty was finished and not much else was going on, the sight of the spring inspired us to take a wash. While we were bathing, we heard voices speaking Vietnamese and guns being loaded behind us, but we were too scared and didn't know what to do, so we just stood there in the water, naked, without turning around, like two dead statues. We told him everything in detail.

Commander Min listened to our story and patted me on the shoulder. "No matter how hot it is, what kind of person takes a bath in the middle of an operation? It was a miracle you didn't get killed. God saved you again, eh? Thank God." The commander's words suddenly made me think there must be something else to the story that we didn't know.

Min told us the rest of the story he had heard from the two Vietcong deserters. That afternoon, while the rest of the company had been urging surrender through the loudhailer at the main entrance of the cave, the Vietcong inside had snuck out through the back entrance. As they were fleeing, they had seen two Korean soldiers taking a bath, and had been about to shoot us, but then decided that two of them would stand guard while the other 14 got away, and they would shoot us afterwards. When all their fellow soldiers had left, these two Vietcongs had aimed at us and pulled the trigger, but both their guns had misfired. They had run off in the direction of their comrades, but for some reason, after regrouping with the others elsewhere on Chai Mountain, they had felt inspired to surrender and turn themselves in. They had told their comrades that they were going down to the village for food, but had made their way through that treacherous mountainside at 11pm to come to us instead.

After the commander had told us everything he had heard from them through the interpreter, he looked at me and said, "God saved you once again." I felt so relieved, even happy, to finally be able to solve all the day's mysteries, and I could not help but look up at the heavens and thank God Almighty with my whole heart and spirit, for saving my life once again.

After hearing the whole story, I was able to understand what had happened behind us when we were bathing in the spring. God Almighty, who holds me as the apple of His eye and protects my life, and the Lord who loves me, caused the enemy guns to misfire when they were trying to shoot Sergeant Yoo and me. Because the two Vietcong had surrendered, they were able to confirm what had happened, leaving no room for doubt. I strongly felt that God – the owner of all life – had saved them both, as well as us. I was extremely moved after realizing all this.

'It's incredible that I'm alive! Wow, today would have been my last day on earth.' I was amazed – stupefied, almost – thanking God and thinking about how God and Jesus my Lord had saved me once again. My eyes welled up with tears of gratitude. 'Today, the angel of death might have claimed my life through the Vietcong,' I thought, 'but I was saved. How could He save me in such a place as this?' My body, and even my soul and spirit, were overwhelmed with joy and gratitude.

The company commander told us to talk to the two Vietcong deserters, and asked us to check if we recognized their faces. Of course, we hadn't seen their faces, but after hearing them explain what had happened, I was sure it was them. They didn't recognize us either, since we had our backs to them in the spring, but they understood who we were and wanted to talk to us. They were happy to meet us face to face, and we all shook hands and embraced each other.

They looked at our faces, especially mine, and we looked at them. They were our enemies, but after surrendering, they didn't look like enemies anymore. They had almost killed us, and our fellow soldiers could have killed them. They seemed amazed to see us, and couldn't stop smiling and touching us, patting our shoulders or hugging us.

I was overwhelmed to think that these men, who had been trying to kill us, were moved to the point of coming here and turning themselves in. My parents, my brothers, even my fellow soldiers were not the ones protecting me: it was only God Almighty, in whom I placed my trust. He listened to the ceaseless prayers of my parents and brothers, and protected me once again.

It was a miracle that these two Vietcong had faced many dangers to approach the enemy base in the middle of the night to turn themselves in. God inspired them to surrender, and through that, God showed me how much He loves me, how He cherishes my life, and how He watches with eyes like fire to protect me even by miraculously making the guns misfire when I was facing certain death. Without meeting those Vietcong, my life still would have been saved but I wouldn't have known what had happened and how much I had to thank God for.

Ah, this day
would have been my last
on Honba mountain
an angel of death
came with the Vietcong
and pulled the trigger,
but the Almighty,
whom I love and who loves me,
made the gun misfire
He turned the barrel around.

If they hadn't confessed
how would I have known?
Heaven touched their hearts,
made them turn themselves in,
made them open their mouths,
and let me know
the secret
how much the Almighty loves me
how much He protects me

Because of my love
for my enemies' lives,
the Almighty showered me with
the grace of life
God made me realize first
so that I can tell everyone
how deeply God loves
each and every life
just as He loves my life.

How could I forget this grace?
How could I keep silent
and not tell all the world
this story between
God Almighty and I?
With this story in my heart forever,
until the day I die,
loving the Almighty
will be my joy.

It had not been my plan, but God's. I realized that because I loved the lives of my enemies and did not aim my gun at them, God rewarded me according to my deeds so that when my enemy aimed a gun at me, it came to nothing. There were many similar incidents I went through during those fierce operations.

I have shared deep stories from the battlefield like this one with many people, and now God has inspired me to write them in a book as a testimony to everyone. Even though each person is in a different situation and stage of life, and even though we cannot confirm everything that God does for us, I can assure all of you that the Lord of Creation protects each and every life from various dangers.

After confirming everything that had happened that day, the company commander was surprised to hear what God had done, I was surprised, and the Vietcong who surrendered were also surprised. Miracles take place wherever the Almighty shows his power. The commander, Sergeant Yoo, the Vietcong, and I were all intensely relieved to find the answers to all the day's questions.

Since we didn't share a language, I used hand gestures to tell the Vietcong that God had saved us and that's why we were all there together, alive. They couldn't fully understand what had happened that day, but realizing that we were all believers seemed to bring the pieces together for them too. They kept saying, "cảm ơn, cảm ơn," or 'thank you' in Vietnamese. Commander Min also smiled at us and seemed pleased.

This experience solidified my belief that God would protect my life in whatever kind of extreme difficulties I found myself. If God had performed the miracle of saving my life but had not moved the Vietcong to surrender, that incident would have remained a mystery to me.

People don't realize, or don't believe, how the invisible God helps them and spares their lives, and many say instead that their ancestors or idols helped, or that they survived through luck or skill. Yet, only the one who created life can control it. We are alive today because the Author of Life loves each life. God works in secret, so who can know His deeds? He works invisibly, so we cannot see or know. Still, even animals know when people save them from death many times. In the same way, a person must realize that God, the Lord of life, saved them, when they reflect on many incidents. God made me experience all this and realize first, so that I would testify and everyone would surely know that it was God Eternal who saved us from death.

The surrender of the two Vietcong soldiers was suddenly the hot topic around the platoon and company. People asked Sergeant Yoo and me to tell them the story, and they could barely believe it. They couldn't deny anything we said, though, because the two Vietcong had said the same. Miraculously, the whole company believed and even confessed that God had done this. No one thought of it as a coincidence or as unremarkable; rather, it was an opportunity for them to entrust their futures to Heaven.

The company commander Min never saw me as someone ordinary. He had seen me cheat death many times, even in truly deadly situations on operation, and he gave me the nickname of 'god' or 'son of god.'

INSPIRATION ABOUT THE COMPANY COMMANDER

I am going to tell you a story that happened twenty years after I returned from Vietnam. I was sharing this testimony, along with other stories, with more than tens of thousands of people who followed and learned from me. I spoke of God's grace and the time I took a bath on Honba Mountain and the Vietcong were going to shoot me but ended up surrendering of their own volition. Some Military Academy cadets and graduates who heard my story went to meet Commander Min who had led the third company. I heard that he became a Major General after returning from Vietnam.

When they told Min the story that they had heard from me, he said that he remembered it well, even though it took place long ago, because he often talked to the soldiers in his command about Vietnam. He recounted the story again, in detail. Those men were so moved after hearing the story again and the story felt so vivid that they too testified about this incident before crowds of people. I was able to write the story here using references they shared with me.

During my time in Vietnam, Min told me that it was his dream to become a general, and he asked me to pray for him several times. I also remember him speaking seriously on the need for no allies to be killed without corresponding military gains, and the impact that such an event could have on his plans to become a general.

Although he was ranked far above me, we were quite close. We were both believers, and he often asked me about spiritual things, since that was my domain. I would tell him about what the future held and other revelations from God. He saw what I experienced on operation, and did not think of me in an ordinary way, but as a man of foresight.

Around 1994, I heard he was at the school under the ROK Army Training & Doctrine Command. I wanted to see him, so I went there with my brother

Yong-Seok and some other friends. After we sent him a message requesting a meeting, he invited us in. He recognized me immediately and we drank tea and spoke for half an hour.

I had been travelling all over Korea holding religious assemblies, which he seemed happy to hear. He said that even after becoming a general, he had no free time and was tied up with working and being on call for his boss. He said it was great that I had freedom to do great things. I told him that it was so good to see him in person, after becoming a general, especially when I had prayed for him so much back in the day. He asked me to come and see him often, so I said I would attend the Vietnam War Veterans' reunion and we shook hands.

As we were saying goodbye, I felt a passing inspiration about his death. I thought, 'He seems healthy, he's not going to die any time soon,' but I didn't brush off this inspiration. I thought to myself that I should meet him often in the future and help him build his faith in God. I hoped to talk with him more deeply at our next meeting. I suggested we take a photo together to remember the occasion, and he agreed. After that we left.

I attended the Vietnam War Veterans' reunion several times following that and met up with those I had served with in Vietnam. I didn't see General Min, but some who participated in those events passed on updates. I heard Min was happy about what I was doing and had said, "Jeong stood out in Vietnam because of his life of faith and the signs that God was with him. Even now, he is doing great work in the world."

One day, the Vietnam War Veterans' reunion was held in Seoul and General Min also attended. He drank soju as if it were cold water. I didn't drink.

I have never drunk a glass of alcohol in my life, and I don't even like the smell. He said that I had to drink and not be a spoilsport, since we hadn't seen each other for so long, but I wouldn't drink with them even if we had been apart for 30 years. Everyone kept pouring soju in my glass, so I hid a bowl under the table and tipped the soju out while no one was watching, in order not to spoil the mood. They were happy to keep pouring me more, thinking I was drinking it.

People who don't drink often end up in awkward situations, with those around them trying to make them drink. Some of these drinkers resort to all kinds of methods, such as getting upset and pouring alcohol over the head of the one refusing to drink. It's not something worth fighting over or getting angry about. No matter how much someone loves to drink, they shouldn't force others to drink against their will. I really can't understand why drinkers treat non-drinkers in that way.

You often hear that moderate drinking is good for one's physical and mental health and wellbeing, but it's rare that people finish with only moderate drinking. They start off moderately, but later it becomes a habit to drink and get drunk. Whether you drink a little or a lot, it is harmful to your health. It is also emotionally harmful. After drinking, people play drunken games, they fight with their friends, spouses, parents, bosses or subordinates, and they embarrass and hurt each other. They make many mistakes because of alcohol, which non-drinkers avoid, and they suffer a great deal of harm. Alcohol is not only bad for one's health, it can be fatal.

Watching them drinking at the Veterans' reunion, I saw that they enjoyed it but overindulged. I thought, 'Even if they can tolerate that much alcohol and they're used to it, it's going to affect their health.' General Min grinned at me and told me I didn't know what I was missing out on, because alcohol was delicious and I should enjoy it even as I lived my life of faith. He insisted that after drinking, I would feel great, so I'd be able to preach better and make others happy too. I was sincerely worried about him and about the state of his health, considering how much he drank.

When everyone got drunk, they started bringing up stories of the war and of their comrades in Vietnam 30 years before. However, as the evening progressed, some of them got really drunk, raising their voices and cursing for no reason.

I wanted to go to those reunions more often, but the meetings were not very meaningful, and I was busy with my work, so I stopped attending. They kept inviting me, though, and told me just to come even if I didn't drink.

A few years later, one of my fellow veterans, Sergeant Jeong, called me with news that General Min was in the hospital, and asked me to go and visit him. Jeong had been an administrator in the Third Company in Vietnam. I asked why Min was in hospital, and he said it seemed like a stomach or liver problem, possibly liver cancer. I was shocked, and said I would try to visit. It was the alcohol that brought on his suffering and death. I remembered how much he had enjoyed drinking during the Vietnam War Veterans' reunion.

I was touring all over Korea holding assemblies, so although I wanted to visit him, I wasn't able to. Later, I heard that he had passed away. I attended his funeral at Daejeon National Cemetery with my fellow soldiers, and saw his coffin lowered into the ground. A few years previously when I met him at the military academy, I had a feeling about his death, and that day had arrived. I realized it at that moment.

When the inspiration about his death touched me, I think he was already in a bad state. He died leaving regrets, and his body returned to dust without even reaching the age of 60. He survived the violence of war, yet he could not overcome the disease that led to his death. It seemed like an empty life. He reached the rank of two-star general, which people say is more difficult to do than catching hold of a star in the sky, but he failed to hold on to his health.

He was a great commander and leader of my company in Vietnam. I thought of those days, and unexpected tears came. It was the regard and affection I had felt, from him and for him, that moved me like that, along with our interwoven memories. Who can say in advance when a man will die? Now, that inspiration was long gone, so I prayed for his spirit. If his body had remained alive, I could have spoken with him, asked him this and that about Vietnam, and written here about a brave company commander, but the time was gone, and I felt regret.

I spent some years trying to find Sergeant Yoo, who had survived bathing in the spring on Honba Mountain with me 25 years before. I never did manage to find him. I think perhaps he died before the age of 50. I remember I was worried about his health in Vietnam, while reading his palm.

FORESEEING THE FUTURE

I often talked with my fellow soldiers about life, back when we were in Vietnam, and I used to tell them what I was inspired about concerning the future. They liked that, and the squad leader and all the soldiers nicknamed me 'Chaplain Jeong.' They often came and talked to me about their problems or their families. I was also curious, and asked them a lot of questions: "What will you do after you're discharged? What philosophy do you live by? Have you ever dated someone? Do you have children? Are you religious?" And I gave them what answers I had about life.

I realized many things through those conversations, because I had lived an ascetic life prior to joining the army. So I had a lot of stories to share, and could also clearly see certain things about the future. They were especially curious when I spoke about the future, and consulted me like a fortune-teller. They liked to have their palms read and I understood their psychology, so I read their palms using what I knew about them.

One day, Sergeant Yoo asked me to read his palm. I warned him,
"If you drink, you will die young. Your only chance at a long life is if you quit drinking alcohol." Looking at his palm, I told him that he might not live past 50 if he continued to drink.
He replied, "I am also thinking I might not live that long. But will I be prosperous?"
"Based on the palm lines, it doesn't look good, but if you believe in God and Jesus like me, things will turn out better."
At the time, I read his palm hoping to convince him to drink less, but he said he couldn't live without it. He probably ended up dying young, and his spirit went to the spiritual world of alcoholics.

The squad leader also held out his hand and said that since he heard I can read palms well, I should read his future. I was only doing it for fun, but I couldn't really reject him without causing offence, and he could easily make my life miserable, so I read his palm. I couldn't tell him everything I sensed about his life, but I told him his life-line was short and he could live longer if he stopped drinking. I told him that his future would be difficult and he would definitely need God's blessing, so he should believe in God to escape the rough cliffs of life and walk a smooth path. He replied that death would be preferable to not drinking, and asked me to pray for him to receive blessings instead, since he couldn't quit drinking and believe in Jesus.

Then Corporal S, a new recruit, asked me to read his palm and tell him what he should do after being discharged from the army. I said that I was such an expert I didn't even need to see his hand.

Since the Corporal had great artistic talent, I told him his life would go well if he took up painting. He said that he had done some painting before, as a hobby, but if he became an artist he would starve to death.

Even though he kept asking if there was something else, I told him he should be a painter. I said I couldn't see any other profession from his palm, so he sighed morosely, not knowing what to do with his future.

I was thinking about them all 25 years later and made efforts to track them down. I couldn't find my old squad leader: I had told him to drink less and live longer, but it appeared he had not listened and had drunk himself to death. He probably went to a place for alcoholics after his death.

I did find Corporal S: he had become a successful painter. Although he was my junior, I spoke respectfully and praised him. "S, you became successful. I'm glad it wasn't just me. I'm so happy you took my advice and it worked out so well." He was covered in paint drops as we shook hands enthusiastically. We reminisced about our time together in Vietnam and he was moved to tears.

He thought he would starve as a painter, but because of what I had said, he had continued to paint. He ended up becoming a famous artist in the southwestern region in Korea and receiving accolades and honors. Sadly, when I called him a few years later, he was in hospital after failing to take care of his health, and I was not able to speak with him.

He has since passed away. There is a saying that goes: once a man can afford to eat well, the time has come for him to leave the earth. Indeed, such a life is meaningless. Riches and fame are as empty as flowers that bloom in spring and then wither and die.

A life is so precious it cannot be traded even for the whole earth, yet people don't value and care for their lives enough, and so many lives are lost from lack of wisdom and effort. It's such a pity.

Some people face many twists and turns in life. I especially counsel such people to pay careful attention to their health and not drink. I, myself, have invested in studying health and medicine because it is my mission to save lives – both bodies and spirits. Spiritual inspiration, like a sixth sense, often allows me to discover and/or treat injuries and health conditions. Through this, I have foreseen many issues that would have become fatal, and prevented many deaths. God uses me to save people through this kind of inspiration.

IF A LIFE WAS SAVED BY GRACE, THAT GRACE MUST BE REPAID WITH THAT BODY

First and foremost, the grace that saved one's life must be repaid. If it is not repaid when you are alive, it cannot be repaid after death. The most valuable and meaningful thing for a person to do is to escape death and use that body to repay the grace of being given life. When you receive grace, you should repay it with words or actions right away, without delay.

That is the appropriate response to receiving grace.

Let's say that someone rescued a man, the breadwinner of his family, from death. The man should thank his rescuer and do something to repay that grace, then the rescuer will be glad and feel his efforts were worthwhile. However, say that he died without repaying the grace. If his son later finds out and thanks the rescuer and tries to repay him, the rescuer will probably say, "Did I save your life? You don't need to do this."

The same is true for each of our lives. The payment God wants for His grace is for the one who was saved to rejoice and love God, and to be thankful to God and to the people who gave their aid. Then, the one who did the saving will receive greater glory and feel satisfied.

Let's say a person receives the grace of life from God, and yet lives an ignorant and ungrateful life without repaying that grace. After he dies, his spirit goes to the spiritual world and there, he thanks God for having saved his body. God would say, "I saved your body those times you would have died, not your spirit. What are you, the spirit, thanking me for?"

If the body receives grace, the body that was saved should give thanks and repay that grace while it is alive. Those who do not give thanks to God cannot receive a better salvation, whether in heaven or on earth.

There are many ways to repay the grace of being saved from death. For myself, I've been preaching about God, and now I am writing this book. As for your own experiences, no one else can share them if you do not. No one but I, myself, can express what I went through and vividly paint a picture of what I did and felt. I am writing these stories not to boast about myself, but to boast about the one who saved my life. In the single second before death,

I wanted desperately to live, so He saved me. Thus, it is only natural, as well as my duty, to share about Him without forgetting the gratitude of that moment.

A man who narrowly escapes death would do anything for the one who saved him, but people forget God's grace. There is a Korean proverb that says, "A man feels differently before going into the restroom and after coming out." This is how people behave toward God.

The Almighty works in secret. When people are saved from death or difficulties, they say their friends helped them, or one of the gods, or their ancestors; or they say it was a coincidence or luck. But if that's what it was, why don't their horoscopes or their friends or ancestors help them live longer, and why would they die young?

The Almighty Creator of our lives knows everything about life and death. Only He who is omnipresent and omnipotent can determine the outcome. Since we were born as human beings — not as animals but as the supreme of all creation — we must realize the will of our Creator and live better, more worthwhile lives.

People wonder: if God is in absolute control of life, why do people die in car accidents, on battlefields, or in other ways before their time? But He who created life does not manage it alone. Parents give birth to a child, but the child has control of his own life. In the same way, God created our lives but we must live them: we must do our responsibility, and God manages only the part that is His responsibility. Thus, a man's life depends on both the actions of the Creator and the man himself.

The misfortune of people dying before their time is caused by themselves or others failing to do their full responsibility toward caring for life. People die unjustly due to the ignorance of themselves or those around them, or die in God's judgement of their own sins or the sins of a generation. The righteous sometimes die for the sins of the people, or following God's will.

People who don't know this, whether believers or not, often lay their resentment before the heavens for unjust deaths, accidents or illnesses. People die for lack of foreknowledge: those who know in advance can avoid death and even fate. God Almighty, ruler over the life and death of man, acts according to each person's deeds. The one who saves life is the one who created it: this knowledge is the advantage in saving the life of oneself or another.

When people know this and treat God accordingly, their lives have that much greater protection. Each person in every nation in the world is the same. That is, everyone on earth has faced either death or extreme difficulty. People should know that God controls life, but helps and saves people based on their own actions. Those who heard my story and learned from me have realized these things and live in that joy, with me. I did not hide the grace heaven afforded me, but I testified and repaid that grace, so God granted me His great power and a mission to do His miracles on a worldwide scale.

If people just keep asking for grace without repaying it, the giver, whether God or man, will not feel moved to give. Anyone who receives God's great grace, including the grace to escape death, but fails to offer glory to God and live for others, will come to ruin in the end. We must all put our lives on the line for the one who saved us and live to repay His grace. I have spoken about God, who I know presides over all life, based on my experiences.

| SUPPORTING THE VIETNAMESE PEOPLE, AND HELPING
OUT WITH THE HARVEST |

IN THE VIETNAM

THRESHING RICE; THRESHING LIFE

WAR   1966-1969

*"God decided the fate
of the battle looking at
the one who fought
His operation of love."*

CHAPTER 6

THRESHING RICE; THRESHING LIFE

THRESHING RICE: AN OPERATION OF LOVE AND PEACE

Our company received an order from the regiment and headed out early one morning on an operation. After travelling for some time by truck, we got out and walked into a village. I didn't know the name of the village: the houses were quite spread out, interspersed with fields, and some were abandoned. The operation was to ambush the enemy that night, so we had to wait for dusk before moving roughly 200 meters forward into the ambush position.

Myeong-Shin Chae, the Commander in Chief of the Korean forces in Vietnam, had directed all Korean soldiers to protect and support the local farmers so they could harvest their crops safely. So we decided to go out early in the day to help the farmers out in the fields harvesting grain.

Whenever the Vietcong needed food, they went down into the villages and stole whatever they wanted, driving the civilians away into larger villages where the Korean troops were able to protect them. It wasn't safe to return to their villages whenever they wanted to, so even when the rice was ready to harvest, the villagers couldn't harvest and thresh it except when the Korean troops were protecting the area.

On the day of this particular operation, the local people had heard we would be operating in their village, so they all showed up to collect their grain and followed us. They cut the ripe grain and threshed it as fast as they could. Our company's four platoons were deployed to wait in some of the vacant houses in the village, so that we could protect the civilians during the day and set up an ambush at night.

1st platoon was headquartered in a house that had no roof because it had been shelled. The floor and walls were cement, and above us was nothing but a clear view of the sky. The platoon members were deployed around the house, and the company kept a rotation of soldiers patrolling around the village during the day, while other soldiers slept in preparation for the night operation.

I was assigned to the platoon headquarters as a grenadier, along with the radioman and the medic. Our platoon leader, second lieutenant J, instructed all of us to take turns napping so that we would get enough sleep before the night operation.

During the rest period, J told us not to talk amongst ourselves or do our own thing. To me, his instructions were: "Don't read the Bible, but sleep for the night operation." But he said it with a smile, knowing that I couldn't help but read the Bible whenever I got the chance.

A young woman came into the house where our platoon was headquartered to thresh her rice, rubbing the heads of grain against the concrete floor with her feet. The soldiers watched her for a while, and asked with a smile, "Is she Vietcong?"

The house actually belonged to her, but the roof had been destroyed by shells, and she had moved somewhere safer, returning only to thresh her rice. She was thankful for the Korean troops protecting the village while she diligently threshed the sheaves of rice by rubbing the grains off with her feet.

Watching her brought up memories of threshing back home, and I wanted to help her. Furthermore, our Commander in chief, Myeongshin Chae, had ordered us not to focus only on fighting the enemy but also to help the local people with the harvest. So I wanted to help even more because helping her was part of the operation. She even reminded me of how I used to thresh barley with my sister and my mother in summer. She almost looked like my sister threshing by herself. She had no special equipment, and was using the somewhat primitive technique of tying the rice in sheaves and rubbing the grains off with her feet. I figured that the farming techniques in Vietnam had lagged behind Korea because of many years of war.

I went to help her, using the more conventional method of slapping the sheaves against the mat, while instructing her to fan away the rice husks with another piece of matting.

After sweating away at the task for more than two hours, I was covered from head to toe in rice husks. The woman seemed entertained by this new method of threshing, although she was also hard at work with her fan. I couldn't stop thinking about my younger sister, Youngja, and the times we had threshed together back home.

| ON THE DAY WE WENT OUT TO SUPPORT THE VILLAGERS, I HELPED
A VIETNAMESE WOMAN TO THRESH MORE THAN TWO SACKS OF RICE |

I really got into the work, as if it was my farm and my rice. The woman smiled and looked over at me from time to time. She was so happy she didn't know what to do. I couldn't tell whether she was happy about the work or about me. Earlier in the day, she was quite wary of us and didn't bother answering any of our questions. But after helping her thresh the rice, her whole attitude changed, from her posture to her facial expression. When asked how she felt about Korean soldiers now, she responded with a thumbs up. She looked about twenty years old.

I ended up threshing more than two bags of rice on that concrete floor while also paying vigilant attention to the situation around me. My whole body ached, especially my back, because I hadn't done that kind of work for a long time. The other soldiers used the time to sleep in preparation for the ambush that night. The courier woke up and asked me, "Aren't you going to rest, Corporal Jeong? You're looking after her like she's your family, which is very kind, but there's nowhere to wash here. Don't you feel uncomfortable?"

I admitted that I felt sorry for her working alone and had helped her while thinking of my own parents and my sister. Although rice is less prickly than barley, it was still very itchy to be completely covered in sweat and prickly husks. The courier joined in and also spent a long time threshing, until he couldn't bear the itchiness any more. We went to clean up and at least wash a little, using canteen water, and I poured the water for him and helped him wash his back.

The other soldiers were well rested, so they got up and walked around, stretching. One of them asked me why I had made myself hot and sweaty and uncomfortable by working so hard. I told him that physical love shouldn't be the only thing we cared about on the battlefield, but we should serve the local people with mental love and joy. The soldiers all cared more about killing as many enemies as possible than showing love to the local people as our commander in chief had directed us. Even on that day, no one except the courier and me had offered assistance, in that operation of peace and love.

The civilians had arrived early in the morning, and by about 3pm they began to collect up what they had threshed into handcarts to move out before the Vietcong became active. The woman I had helped finished the work a few hours earlier than she expected, so she was very pleased and kept saying thank you in Vietnamese. She loaded up her handcart, which I couldn't help her with because I wasn't allowed to go outside the house.

Then she fell serious and warned me to be careful, and told me that a very large number of Vietcong would appear after sunset. I showed her my watch and asked when they would come down the mountain, and she indicated 4 o'clock. We used sign language because I couldn't understand Vietnamese, and she told me cautiously, constantly looking around to make sure no one else could see her.

She had not intended to give us any specific information in the beginning, but her heart was moved by seeing me take on her work as if it were my own. As a sister to a brother, she told me to be careful. I hadn't helped her out of any scheme to get information about the Vietcong – who could have guessed that a small piece of information would carry such significance as to make hundreds of Vietcong disappear like smoke?

Pulling her heavily loaded handcart, she waved back at me, feeling both thankful and hoping that I'd be ok, as if she loved me. That cart was too

| A CIVILIAN WOMAN GAVE INFORMATION ABOUT THE VIETCONG AND
LEFT WITH BAGS FULL OF THRESHED GRAIN |

heavy to easily navigate those unpaved roads, and I wanted to help her push it back to her home, but I could only wish her well. At least she had been able to leave early, and she managed that heavy cart with determination and strength. Talking about her like this makes me think that she might talk about me, too, if she is still alive.

The other civilians who had come along to thresh their grain wrapped up at around 3pm and every single one of them left. We had gone to that village without any special intelligence about the enemy, so the information the woman gave me took on extra significance. I believed what she'd said and immediately reported it to platoon leader J, who reported it to Company Commander Min. Enemy intelligence is like life on an operation, so the company commander, although he was surprised, changed the plan right away.

At 4pm, he made everyone wake up and stand guard. Some Vietcong could have seen us from a distance, so we behaved as though we were withdrawing, and one platoon remained secretly to set up an ambush in a rice paddy on a rise in front of the village, while the others three platoons hid in the back of the village. Without the tip-off, the entire company would have been attacked while still in the center of the village.

At dusk, 2nd platoon reported that the Vietcong had appeared near where they were lying in wait. However, a great number of Vietcong were moving into the village, so we had to suspend the operation. The company commander ordered us to watch them vigilantly without giving away our location. The Vietcong entered the empty village through the road in the front, and during the night, withdrew by a different route. And instead of coming back through the same path, they decided not to come back.

The information the woman had given me was correct, and if we had all been stationed at the front of the village, we would have faced a far greater force than expected and very unfavorable battle conditions. A lot of lives would have been lost.

We could have met with great misfortune that day. I was every bit as thankful, thinking about it, as the woman who thanked me for my help. The thought came to me: 'There really are no freebies. You reap what you sow.' It felt really worthwhile to sweat and work all morning even at the cost of being clothed in rice husks. Barley husks would have been worse, but I was itchy enough to scratch my skin raw as if I had some skin problem, since I wasn't able to wash properly. Still, we were amazingly fortunate not to have engaged with that great number of enemy troops.

Even on the battlefield, you must treat civilians well and not harm them. Strangely, that woman's face had reminded me of my sister, but because she gave us accurate information, we were able to change our ambush strategy, and avoid a bloodbath. It was obvious to me that God and Jesus had protected me once again, moving my heart to think of that woman as my sister so that I would help her and they would speak through her. I can't help but thank God and Jesus who granted me the grace of life when I think back on this story.

THE VIETCONG SOLDIERS WHO USED TO STEAL FOOD LOSE THEIR LIVES

That night, the company commander clearly grasped the situation of that large Vietcong force, and before dawn the next day, he deployed the whole company to the plain closest to the hill where the enemy would appear again. We waited until 3 p.m. without seeing any Vietcong.

The civilians came as they had the previous day and once again disappeared before 4 p.m. after harvesting and threshing their rice, and taking it with them in bags. Enemy soldiers began to gather at the foot of the hill: 30, then 50, then 70, following the path laid out on the hill. Just as the woman had told us the previous day, they camouflaged themselves with grass and branches and crossed over the narrow track in small groups. We couldn't tell if they were local Vietcong or regular forces in the North Vietnamese army, but they gathered in a large, overgrown field at the foot of the mountain like a gathering storm cloud.

As our company waited there, the soldiers were afraid because of the large number of enemies. We couldn't exactly see where they were standing because of the trees in front, but it seemed like there were a lot more soldiers than we could see. The assembled troops were being assigned to different villages and regions and appeared to be going out on operations, as they had the previous night. The number gathered here and there for an hour was enormous. Their tactics usually kept them apart from each other. In fact, even a small number of enemies always seemed to be a lot more when we encountered them. Watching through binoculars, we could see at least 200 troops, but that was without counting those hidden among the trees.

We estimated there were about 500 or 600 enemy soldiers, and when we saw them, we were shocked. It was unusual for so many enemies to move at once. It was like facing a school of fish with just a fishing rod, when a fishing net was absolutely necessary. Company commander Min agreed with those around him that it was time to cast the net. He continued to radio situation reports to regiment headquarters through the battalion, and, seeing the opportunity, called in Phantom fighters (F-4) for CAS (Close Air Support) as well as field artillery fire. The regiment's artillery battalion and the US Air Force Phantom fighters waited on full alert.

Our company was assigned to the hill closest to the enemy, and while monitoring the Vietcong, we directed the remote artillery and air support. We all felt anxious because there were so many enemies. If we had run into them it really would have been a bloodbath. People were saying things like, "I'm scared, there are way too many of them." "Rifles are not going to be enough." "Even grenade launchers and grenades won't give us enough firepower to defeat them." The enemy was about 500 meters away in a straight line, so it was true that the arms we had would not be sufficient.

As the sun began to set behind the high mountains, we could see that even more enemy troops had gathered. Seeing them spread out at the foot of our hill was shocking to us, as we had never seen such an incredible number of enemies at once. Usually the numbers appear greater when the enemy is spread out in smaller groups.

We continued to monitor their movements, as we would need to act quickly before the sun set completely. We could see them gathering closer and closer. Our military tended to use similar tactics to the enemy forces. After a short while, they assembled and appeared to be receiving instructions for an operation.

All of us were glancing at our watches, saying, "Now's the chance, right now!" and anxiously waiting for the Phantom jet. We needed to finish the operation before the sun set. The Vietcong were constantly on the move, so the opportunity would disappear if the bomber was even ten minutes late. Our company commander had quickly assessed the situation based on his battle experience and had reported back to the regiment, but the bomber still hadn't appeared. The whole company was waiting anxiously, making frustrated comments about missing such a good opportunity if they didn't show soon. Every minute felt like an hour as we kept checking our watches.

Suddenly, in an instant, the Phantom jet roared overhead, and in just a few seconds had dropped several bombs in the middle of the enemy ranks. Before we could even hear the whistle of falling bombs, they exploded, sending earth, rocks, bodies of the Vietcong and debris flying 50 meters in the air, like paper caught in a whirlwind. Objects were flying in the wind like a storm. Bodies shot up into the air and torn fragments of clothing flew away. The Phantom swooped again, close to the ground for maximum accuracy, and dropped more bombs before banking sharply into the sky.

We were too caught up in what was happening to even make a sound. The bombing happened too fast for the enemy to move or counterattack in any way, no matter how fast they might have been. They knew nothing about the attack and were caught by surprise and blown up.

One bomb after another, the Phantom was right on target, and the Vietcong were scattered in all directions from the first pass. It somehow made me think of a man lying in wait for a thief to break into his house, and beating him over the head with a cudgel. The bombs made dirt and fire spurt up into the air like a volcano erupting, and bodies and guns

| THE ENEMY CONTINGENT IS BROKEN UP INTO PIECES BY THE AIR STRIKE |

were thrown 30 meters or even up to 50 meters high. Broken bodies and shreds of clothing appeared to float in the air like leaves, and took a long time to fall back to the earth.

After we had gotten over our first shock and as bombs continued falling, we began screaming at this brutal yet stunning scene, no longer concerned about staying hidden. We could scream as much as we wanted, because the enemy had been wiped out.

Where the Vietcong had been gathered was now just a sea of fire, and everything there had turned to ashes in a few short moments. The wind carried the acrid smell of flesh burning. It looked like a different planet: the green landscape had become a desolate wasteland with so many bombs being dropped in just a few minutes. Who would have known that one woman's words could have such an impact?

I wondered if the sins of the Vietcong had brought this on themselves. They stole the crops that the Vietnamese people had tended under fear of death in the midst of a war. We reap what we sow, not only in wartime. I remembered the Korean War, when my family had starved because the North Korean soldiers stole what we harvested. The suffering of hunger is like hell. The Vietcong went from village to village taking all the food, not just once or twice but taking almost everything. I can't imagine the suffering that those farmers went through when they were robbed even of food to survive. They went through the suffering of war, lost their possessions, and starved too. All the young people, men and women, had been dragged away, and all the rest lived in fear of being killed in the night. The people tried even burying their grain or hiding it in other ways, but like evil spirits, the Vietcong found everything and swept it all away. The Vietcong claimed that by taking the villagers' food, they would liberate them and end the war, and that peace would come if all the people followed them. They were not well supplied, so the only way for them to keep fighting was to steal from civilians. Now, instead of stealing food, they were lying in a fiery grave.

The sun finally began to set. After the bombing raid, the artillery unit followed up with shell after shell, burning up the surrounding area in a sea of fire. The sun disappeared and dusk set in. A star shell was used to light up the area like daytime.

In the sky, stars sparkled, and on the ground, flares lit up the area in flashes. The moon, seven days since the new moon, sailed in and out of the clouds, illuminating the earth. Usually the night was filled with bird sounds, but that night was quiet. I guess the birds all got scared off by the bombs. The only sound was the wind whistling across the ground.

Boom! Boom!
Exploding bombs
leaving
stripped trees
bare boughs
in an instant
and leaving lives
as falling leaves in autumn winds

The people
and even the birds
flew away
across the sea and over the mountains
unable to bear the noise

On the earth
the only sounds
are voices carried by the wind

We stayed awake that night, thinking about how many Vietcong had died and how many weapons had been captured. We were more relaxed than usual, even as we stood guard, because no one could approach us through the sea of fire. It was a night my fellow soldiers could sit comfortably and think about home, or talk about their wives and children.

Life
Is created in the blink of an eye
And ends in the blink of an eye

Life
is like falling autumn leaves

196

I saw them today
just fallen leaves

If just one
of those many people
had known what would happen
they wouldn't have suffered
this pointless tragedy

Oh, life
ignorance destroys the chance for a good life,
and kills people in the end

The heart of the one who sees it
aches more
than that of the dead
The fear of death wells up
the more you see that fearful sight

Is it God's judgment
for their deeds?

or is it human cruelty?
or the struggle for freedom?

Is this struggle
the only way to buy freedom?

Oh, it is not
It is not God's way.

Melting down the weapons to war
to make cars,
farm equipment,
household goods,
and for scientific advancement

Taking the body used in war
making it a weapon of love instead,
and loving each other

this is the will of God
and the freedom He granted human beings

In this way freedom comes
freely and naturally
through love

The deeper the night
the deeper the odor penetrates
emanating from a sea of fire

Oh,
the spirits of the dead groan
How did this happen?

They cannot say they lived well
Life is like a falling autumn leaf

There is no guarantee of tomorrow
for a life on the battlefield;
and no guarantee of today

The future is just a fantasy
just a dream
Only God can guarantee the future

Bombs cremated them
those men of war
Even the ashes were scattered in the wind,
and what is left?
When time passes by
even their names
are not remembered

But those who search for God
and love Him,
their names and spirits
remain forever.

When the day dawned, we ate C-ration for an early breakfast and went to investigate the area that had been burned. The bombs and shells had turned the whole area upside down like there had been an earthquake or a volcanic eruption, and the vibrant green trees had all turned to black.

We were spurred on by the thought of collecting many enemy weapons and were expecting to see countless dead bodies, but to our surprise, we could hardly see any. It was hard to find a single corpse. There were large craters 4-7 meters deep where the bombs had fallen, and the dirt that had been thrown into the sky had buried everything underneath it to a depth of 2-3 meters.

The bodies were buried under the soil, with pieces of debris scattered everywhere. Their personal firearms and other weapons were either buried in the soil or broken up and strewn across the landscape by the force of the explosions. The soil was piled up in large mounds as if a bulldozer had turned over all the soil completely, so we weren't able to find any weapons.

The guns we looted were completely unusable: they had been totally destroyed by the heavy shelling. For some guns we found only the barrel, and for others, only the trigger remained. The other soldiers seemed to find it funny, looking at those gun fragments. If metal guns hadn't survived the bombing, there was no chance of finding bodies either. Even of the big trees, only a handful of blackened stumps remained. They all shattered to pieces without a trace.

Although we spent the day searching, the trees were burned up and even the rocks had been destroyed, the ground was turned upside down and all the weapons of war had been dismantled and thrown about. The heat of the tropics and the stink of burning assaulted our senses. We found only a few enemy soldiers still alive, groaning and dying from their wounds. It was a miserable and gruesome sight. We collected only a few weapons that had been abandoned by Vietcong as they fled from positions around the bombed-out area.

Two days earlier, a civilian woman had come to thresh her grain and had told me there were many Vietcong guerillas near that mountain, and her information had ended up being vital to our operation. The other soldiers had thought of love only in terms of sexual love, but I had loved my neighbor as the Bible teaches, with agape love. Our Commander in chief Chae had instructed us to support and serve the locals, but I was the one who acted on his words by volunteering my assistance. Through that, the woman gave me the information that changed the direction of our night ambush and resulted in the bombing operation, whereby we were able to wipe out the Vietcong threat in that area.

In this way, agape love greatly influenced the outcome of the battle. My commanders and fellow soldiers had both laughed at me and scolded me because of my determination not to shoot the enemy but to love them. However, loving both my neighbors and my enemies as the Bible teaches and fighting for peace was greater service to my side than all those who had found fault with me. The Vietcong lost that day because I, a soldier from a different nation, loved their people and their bloodline more than they did.

The Vietcong leaders did wrong. My fellow soldiers, too, did not care about loving and protecting the lives of others, but only cared about the work that was done with guns and violence. God weighed the fate of each side, friend and foe, while looking at my battle of sincere love.

On that day, Company Commander Min did not ignore the information of a subordinate, but valued it like life, discerned the situation correctly and put a plan in place. Then, with the necessary aerial and artillery support, our company successfully took out hundreds of enemy soldiers and weapons without even engaging them in combat.

Of all the operations I participated in during my tours of Vietnam, I cannot recall any other instance where so many enemies were destroyed in one place without even engaging them directly. The operation was a success because there were no losses on our side, and the only disappointment was not being able to capture more weapons or other spoils because they were destroyed or buried in the soil by the bombs and artillery shells. All the soldiers who experienced that operation would remember it vividly like I do.

The woman who had come to thresh her rice was just an ordinary civilian, but her information did more to eliminate the Vietcong who were tormenting the locals than dozens of soldiers with guns could have done. When she heard that the Korean forces had destroyed the Vietcong in that area, she may have thought back to that moment.

The Vietcong who died that night had come into the village many times at night and had stolen food that should have supported the locals for years. But in the end, the Korean army helped the locals and ended their suffering. The woman would have been appalled at her words if she knew that what she said did this. But the result was surely God's judgement on years' worth of oppression by the Vietcong on the civilian population.

| A HELICOPTER LANDING IN THE JUNGLE DURING A
SEARCH OPERATION |

IN THE VIETNAM

IT WAS NO JOKE

WAR 1966-1969

The men vividly saw a scene:
people just about to die
were calling God and struggling
to live. The scene prompted one
thought: 'They call on God
so desperately at the moment
of death when they never
sought Him before.'

CHAPTER 7

IT WAS NO JOKE

AN ARGUMENT LEADS TO DISASTER

We were on a search operation near Chai Mountain, fully armed and marching in single file under the command of platoon leader J. As we marched toward our search location – up steep mountain ridges, through the jungle – we were always careful to keep a distance of 5 or 6 meters between each of us. We had to move stealthily and pay sharp attention because the operation included the ordeal of getting there as well as the task we had been assigned at the destination. There was fog everywhere. We had no path to follow except the grass crushed underfoot by the soldiers before us.

Lee Taeseong, in front of me, was joking around with some soldiers behind him. They must have been doing it to try to stay awake, and I understood how tired they were, but it was really making me feel uncomfortable. "If you don't shut up, I'll tear your tongue out," shouted someone behind me. Lee shouted back, "If you tear my tongue out, I'll break your neck."

| On a search operation in the jungle, the two comrades changed positions after sparring verbally. |

The soldier behind me said, "You whore, if you try anything, I'll break your skull."

"Sure, do whatever you want, if you're prepared to die."

"Bang! I'll shoot you."

They kept arguing.

Lee turned to face me and told me to go ahead of him. I asked why, but he just pushed me in front. He wanted to change positions because he was mad at the guys cursing behind me and wanted to go and fight them, so I and some others tried to reason with him and told him to wait until the operation was over and deal with it then. But he pushed me again and lagged behind so I had no choice but to try to catch up with the soldier in front, climbing the slope as quickly as possible but also not getting too close to him.

Lee and the soldier behind kept joking around, but they were serious too, trading foul insults with each other, saying, "Why don't you just shoot me?" "Yeah? You think I can't shoot?" A second later a gun went off with an ear splitting 'bang!' All of us were on full alert, and we dropped to the ground without a moment's hesitation.

I also dropped to the ground, trying to protect my head. But already before I dropped, I heard a bullet passing by me. When a person gets shot, they don't feel it right away. I had this feeling that I was the one who'd been shot. Lying face down on the ground, I reached up and felt the back of my head. Something felt wet on my fingers. 'I've been shot!' I removed my helmet to check again, but I discovered that it was only sweat and not blood. My heart pounded violently with shock.

THE MARCHING SOLDIERS DROPPED TO THE GROUND IN UNISON ON
HEARING A GUNSHOT. COMRADE LEE, WHO HAD BEEN SHOT, SCREAMED.

At that moment, I heard someone groaning behind me and turned to look. Lee was thrashing around, tearing up grass and dirt and shouting. He had been shot just a few seconds after we changed positions. He was going crazy and pointing his gun at all of us, as if we were the enemy. I was terrified because each gun was loaded with 21 bullets when we were out on operation. I couldn't tell where he'd been shot, but he had definitely been shot and had collapsed on the ground. His screams echoed off the mountain. The enemy would have aimed for the head or the chest, so I guessed he had been shot in one of those two places.

The medic was next to me but was hesitating to go any closer. I yelled at him to hurry, and he said he couldn't because Lee was waving his gun around. The other soldiers didn't want to go anywhere near Lee either because if an enemy attack had started, we would be much easier targets for grenades and bullets if we were all in one spot. I told the medic that I would follow him if he went first.

Keeping low, the medic crawled to Lee and first took his gun off him, as he'd been trained to do. I followed the medic to hold on to Lee, but I couldn't hold him down and shouted at the others to come and help. They didn't want to move for fear of grenades, but when I kept shouting, a couple of them eventually came. We grabbed Lee's hands and feet and removed his helmet. He had been shot in the head, and his helmet was full of blood. The bullet had gone through the helmet, pierced his forehead, went through the brain, and exited above his right ear. Every time he shouted, blood spurted up out of the hole in his head. The ground was soaked with blood, and the air reeked of it.

The medic applied first aid, wrapping his head in bandages, but the blood quickly soaked through. Lee's face had swollen up in a moment and turned black and blue already, and his head looked like it was almost falling apart. He kept screaming and struggling against us, making horrible noises like a roaring tiger.

After the medic had applied first aid, the platoon leader ordered us back to our positions to keep watch for the enemy, but the sight in front of me was so pitiful and wretched I could barely look at anything. The other soldiers lay down in position, avoiding eye contact with each other.

"GOD, PLEASE SAVE ME!"

Lee called his mother, screaming for her to save him, clutching at the grass and tearing up the ground until his fingernails were torn and bleeding. It even seemed like his fingers were broken.

I yelled at him as he thrashed around, calling his name: "Lee Taeseong! Can you hear me? It's Myeongseok." I grabbed his bloody hand and held it, choking over the words. "We trained together back in Korea- I was number 9 and you were number 10, remember? We ate together, laughed together, and slept in the same barracks. How can I just watch you dying?"

"You lived a good life but you didn't believe in Jesus. I told you that you had to prepare for death, whether your life was long or short. I asked you to come to church, but you refused. Still, I remember that you cleaned my weapon while I was at church, and I was thankful and shared my bread with you."

Lee heard me and understood, but kept crying out for help.
"You were shot in the head. You're dying. What's the point of calling your mother or calling for a doctor? They will be too late – no one can help you.

Just call God. Ask God to save you – and I will too." Like this, I told him everything I wanted to say.

After that he started calling God, again and again, through tears and groaning: "God, save me!" I also raised my voice and prayed aloud, snot and tears running down my face, pleading to God to save him with all the soldiers listening close by. He was so close to death, and there was nothing that could be done for him. I prayed and repented to God for not evangelizing Lee earlier when he still had time.

His head was bandaged and swollen with the bandage now soaked in blood. I held his head in both my hands and earnestly pleaded with God for his life. I absolutely believed that even someone who was certain to die could be brought back to life if God intervened. Lee cried out to God in tears, and I believed God would listen to his cries. My heart was suddenly hot, and I received an answer that God would save him.

Right away I told Lee, "You're not going to die." He heard me and calmed down, holding my hand, so I told him confidently, "It will hurt. You'll be in pain in the hospital, but you won't die."

"God heard our earnest prayers and tears. All the soldiers prayed for you with tears. You won't die, you will surely live. I heard God's voice tell me you won't die. So don't worry."
"Thank you, God. Thank you," Lee said.

The soldiers with us couldn't help but get emotional on hearing him crying out to God so loudly that the mountains echoed with it. He was struggling and beseeching God at the brink of death, so it made them think about how people who are dying seek God so desperately even after never calling Him once in their lives.

I could hear some of them crying. Although we die in different places and situations, everyone dies eventually. Will they only call God then, after never seeking Him in life? The answer is yes – everyone calls God before death.

His groans were heartrending. I couldn't imagine how much pain he must have been in. He was growing weaker and weaker, the sound of his voice dying away, but he wanted to talk, so I asked him what he wanted to talk about. He said he wanted to make a will. I had to put my ear next to his face to hear him. He said his mother was all alone and he was worried about her, and he burst into tears. He also said he had a fiancée back home, but he wasn't sure if she had stuck around.

He asked me to pass on a message to her: "I loved you until the day I died." But I told him he wasn't going to die because God told me He would save him, so I said he didn't need to make a will. I told him there would be suffering but he would survive in the end, and I told him to keep calling on God even in the hospital and never stop praying until he had recovered fully.

Still, anyone who saw the guy would have said he had zero chance of living. He had lost an incredible amount of blood from the head wound, and even worse than that, the fog blanketing the mountain was stopping the medical helicopter from evacuating him. The helicopter couldn't locate us and wandered back and forth in the sky for 20 anxious, agonizing minutes before it was finally able to land.

I and seven other soldiers carried his limp and slippery body to the helicopter. Every groan from his lips made our hearts ache. At least he seemed to be in less pain after we had prayed for him, so he wasn't screaming and thrashing about any more. It was just 50 meters to the helicopter, and we had no stretcher, so the eight of us formed a stretcher with our hands to carry him. Once we got him on board, the helicopter took off immediately.

After Lee left, barely alive, the whole platoon felt like we were at a funeral. We were all very anxious and feeling empty. Everyone said he would probably die on the way to the hospital, considering the severity of his injuries.

Back at base, after we had finished the operation, I asked the soldiers who had been behind me what had happened. They were whispering a lot and giving off a kind of strange vibe, but I couldn't tell if Lee had been shot by the enemy or by the guys he'd been messing around with. They told me I was better off not knowing. Even though I hadn't seen it myself, I knew that this accident had happened because of their squabbling. Anyone could tell just from looking at their faces.

After the accident, the soldiers in my squad remained in shock for hours. I was even more tormented because I was the one who had taken care of Lee up close. The soldiers who knew what had really happened were so upset and angry, but they didn't want to cause more problems and they were afraid of the one who shot Lee, so they didn't say anything.

That accident came up amongst those of us who had been there, even after we were discharged. Some of the men said that after all the time had passed there was no use assigning blame for what had happened. "Lee was in the wrong and the shooter was in the wrong," they said, "people shouldn't go overboard and say reckless things when they joke around."

Those two guys had been friends, but they were often abusive in their humor. It's not that the soldier was so evil he would shoot someone just for goading him to do it, but I think that when people get upset they can lose control of their actions.

"Hey, bitch!
If you come after me,
I'm not gonna do nothing."

Yeah?
And if you come after me?
What then? What you gonna do?
Pussy, dumbass.

"I'm coming
Gonna smash your face in"

"If you smash my face
I'll snap your neck"

This foul language
Getting worse and worse

Soldiers listening in try to intervene:

"We're on an operation

What do you think you're doing?

We don't want to listen to this

Stop now"

Soldiers in front and behind

Try to stop them

But those two

Slander each other

"That bitch pissed me off

He cussed me out"

The contradiction is that

These close friends

Enjoy throwing profanities at each other

They get a thrill from it

I wish they'd do that after the operation was over

After we returned to base

The soldier in front of me says
"That bitch,
He acts like he's better than me
I can't let this go"

He's usually not like this
But when he's upset, he snaps
He shoves me toward the front
And moves behind me

The man behind,
His hot temper comes out
He speaks sharply, with anger
"I'm gonna shoot you"

From the front
"Do you want to shoot me so bad?
Then why don't you shoot?"

From the back
"Do you think I can't shoot you?"

218

From the front
"Ok, go ahead!"

From the back
"Are you sure?
You got nothing else to say?"

Two men
Both upset

Both murderous with hatred
Emotions running high
From the front
"Fine!"

From the back
"You told me to shoot, so watch me!"

-- Bang! --

A fool

Shot a man who told him to
Another fool
Told an angry man to shoot

One shot because of anger
Another was shot because of anger
He probably thought, 'He'll never shoot'
So he said it
Who would think he'd really get shot?

The other soldiers
Not knowing what had happened
Thought they were all facing death
And being attacked by the enemy
Fear stopped their hearts
Cut years from their lives

In fact
That disgraceful incident
Was just the result
Of two fools

This is a lesson

I will remember forever

If you hate,

You will murder

You will kill someone

During the time I had spent in training, living with Lee, I had encouraged him to believe in Jesus and live a life of faith, but he said it wasn't for him. In hindsight, it was more necessary for him than anyone. They say a man swept away in a flood gains sudden strength and can hold on to the smallest straw. People really don't know how much strength is found in believing in the Savior sent from Heaven. At that time, he was lucky that I was there and he didn't die, but until then he had been reluctant to believe in God and Jesus, and on the day of his death, he ran out of luck and suffered a major accident.

Those who meet a person of heaven can ride on the wings of heaven's fortune. From my own experience, I can say that those who followed and took action upon God's Word succeeded, while those who did not suffered misfortune.

Not only the soldiers in my platoon but also my company knew about the pure life of faith that I lived. All of them, even the company commander, nicknamed me 'the army chaplain.' I always talked to the other soldiers about God, encouraging them to live a life of faith, but they refused. You might think that soldiers on a battlefield would be more likely to seek God and believe in Him because of their fear, but it wasn't like that.

Mainly soldiers wanted to drink more, sleep around and do everything their hearts desired – even more so because they didn't know when they might die. They didn't want to believe in Jesus because then they'd have to stop doing those things. They even asked me if they could still go to heaven if they believed in God but also drank excessively, played around and lived selfish, self-centred lives. It was really hard to convince them to live a life of faith when they had that kind of mindset.

When I met them again 25 years later, those who hadn't lived a life of faith then still didn't, those who had liked smoking and drinking then still liked smoking and drinking, and some of them were dying of gastric, lung or liver cancer.

Some of the soldiers who were heavy drinkers during the war were still heavy drinkers after – drinking hard liquor was as easy as eating rice for them, but they ended up dying of gastric or liver cancer. Every time I attended another Vietnam veterans' reunion, more of them were missing because they had died.

Those who lived recklessly when faced with death on the battlefield got used to such a life, and continued in those habits afterward. Just like that, if you ignore the future and the consequences of your actions just because you're in a difficult situation, you will have regrets later.

The Bible says: 'Those who sow with tears will reap with songs of joy.' I endured that difficult time while sowing the seeds of life, and I have lived such a rewarding life. I have travelled around the world, saving lives with joy and reaping the harvest of life. Glory to God in Heaven, and peace and joy to people on earth: that's why I'm writing this book from my corner of the world.

On the day Lee was shot, I deeply realized that God watches over especially those who believe in, love and serve Him, as their guardian.

That particular search operation lasted one week in the Chai Mountain area. We had several skirmishes with the enemy, some big and some small, but we wrapped everything up with no lives lost and returned to base.

| COMMEMORATING WITH THE SOLDIERS OF THE WHITE HORSE WHO WENT OUT TOGETHER. (AUTHOR: THIRD FROM THE RIGHT |

IN THE VIETNAM WAR 1966-1969

LOVE HIM!

*"Love. You must love him.
Then you will live
and he will live."*

| CHAPTER 8 |

LOVE HIM!

THE VIETCONG FOUND AFTER A WEEK'S SEARCH OPERATION

Sareo Mountain, just behind Chai Mountain, was a Vietcong stronghold and military base. We were often sent on search operations in that area.

On one of those occasions, Battalion Commander Lee Young-woo led the First battalion on an operation deep in the mountains. The swamps in the Chai Mountain area were thick with weeds, and night brought dark clouds of blood-sucking mosquitos to torment us.

After the day's work was done, each soldier slept with a mosquito net in the camp, but these feisty jungle mosquitoes would bite us from under a field bed, which usually doesn't poke easily even with a spear. Soldiers who toss and turn a lot in their sleep would sometimes kick their arms or feet out of the mosquito net. When that happened, mosquitoes would bite their arms and legs and suck their blood until they even looked skinnier.

After an exhausting day of work, the soldiers slept soundly, not knowing the mosquitos were sucking their hearts dry or making their legs fall off. It was like the mosquitos made us bleed because they hated the bloody mess us soldiers were making. In any case, the war was no hardship to the mosquitos. They were well fed.

We stayed in inhabitable swamps full of disease-ridden, stagnant water – only a mosquito would choose to live in such a place, but we were stuck there because of the war. That place was so hellish I still can't forget about it decades later: when I think of Vietnam, my first thought is of the mosquitos. Even if I had a nostalgic desire to visit Vietnam again, the thought of being bitten by all those mosquitos just makes me shudder.

When life is hopeless, people still try to endure because they want to live. I felt sorry for the Vietnamese people, stuck in that mosquito-infested land, and for our enemies, facing the daily struggle of mosquitos and other battles out there in the jungle.

Third company searched from the base of Chai Mountain to the peak for a whole week but couldn't find any Vietcong, only traces of them having been there. The other company out on an operation had some skirmishes with the enemy and therefore could report having achieved something, but ours had not, so our company decided to go back and search where we had already been.

Our four platoons were positioned like a net, lining up horizontally by squad, moving down the mountain in search of the enemy. The sun was setting as we slowly descended to the seventh ridge, so Commander J ordered us to set up tents and begin the night watch.

The squad worked quickly, hoping to pitch our tents before darkness fell, but it was difficult to find space on the steep slope, littered with rocks and trees. Some of them ended up pitching their ponchos and tents on top of rocks. That done, we took out our C-ration (combat rations) to eat.

Back in Korea, we hadn't eaten well because our families were poor, and even in the army, the situation wasn't much different. But the meat we got in the C-rations in Vietnam was fantastic. I weighed 60 kg on entering the army, but because of the better diet I put on 5 kg.

In the training camp, in Nonsan, Korea, we got pork soup once a week. We could see some oil floating in the soup, but I guess the pork ran away because we never saw any. Even then, we all looked forward to pork soup day like looking forward to one's birthday. Soldiers in the training camp often stated their two desires as eating their fill and sleeping to their heart's content.

We all envied the cooks like we envied the KATUSA (Korean Augmentation To United States Army), who worked alongside the US military. They got to eat as much as they wanted and slept a lot, too.

Once, when pork soup day rolled around, I found a miraculous piece of pork floating in my bowl. After a quick prayer of thanks, I stuffed it in my mouth and chewed, so no one could steal it from me. It was the best pork in the whole world.

In Vietnam, on that operation, we had expended a lot of energy climbing around the mountain through rocks and jungle, so the soldiers were stuffing down their C-ration, looking like they might burst. Several soldiers, including me and Park Jung-bae, kept a lookout as the others set up tents and ate.

At that moment, Park said in an urgent tone, "The Vietcongs are down there!"

"Where?" I asked.

"See there? Going up the valley."

Looking down the valley 100 meters below, I could see tree leaves moving, and when I looked more closely, there were quite a few armed enemy soldiers hiding behind rocks and trees and climbing up the side of the valley in the dwindling light.

We immediately reported this to the squad leader. The other squad members stared nervously down the valley. They were definitely enemy soldiers down there. They must have seen us moving around the mountain during our operation, and they were sneaking back to the area we had just searched under the cover of dusk. The Vietcong had outsmarted us, leading us on a dance without our realizing it.

After searching for an entire week, we hadn't caught even a glimpse of them in the dense jungle, so that sighting carried with it the excitement of finally meeting them. It appeared that a small Vietcong force was fleeing the path of our grand operation.

PRAYING FOR ENEMY LIVES

Right away, our squad leader reported to platoon leader J that the enemy was headed up the valley 100 meters away, keeping to the shadows, warning that we had only a limited window of opportunity to catch them. J gave immediate firing orders and the squad leader responded like lightning. Park was instructed to fire the automatic rifle, and I was to fire the grenade launcher in even bursts in front and behind the enemy. The other soldiers were to deliver concentrated fire, except those with grenades, since we were too far away to use them.

As we prepared to unleash concentrated firepower on them, the Vietcong just continued up the valley, knowing nothing.

We could see only about ten of them because the rest were invisible beneath the leaves. The Vietcong might have felt safely hidden, thinking only of crossing the mountain as quickly as possible and not considering, in their haste, that they had been outsmarted. We were like a hawk with its sights trained on a pheasant, as the pheasant wiggled under the shelter of a pine tree with its head down, desperately clinging to the illusion of invisibility.

I couldn't help but feel pity for them. 'The enemy on the battlefield cannot escape this fate in the end. Even though they eluded us for a few days, now they will be caught. Although they are my enemy, their lives are precious just as mine is.' I thought. It became impossible to aim my weapon directly at the enemy's chest – it felt like aiming at my own chest. With only a few seconds left before opening fire, I prayed to God for their lives.

When we were ready, the squad leader made the call to open fire. I aimed my grenade launcher over their heads, blowing up rocks instead of enemies, the explosions booming through the valley. Park's automatic rifle fire was, however, right on target.

The attack was so unexpected that the Vietcong couldn't get off a single shot. They collapsed with bullet wounds, or fled despite them, or rolled this way and that way trying to avoid being hit, or tried to hide in the foliage like a wounded tiger. Some thought they were hiding behind rocks, but since they didn't know what direction we were shooting from, they were easily shot and killed.

If the Vietcong had known of the attack just ten seconds beforehand, they would have survived it. Many deaths would be avoidable if people knew the future. Likewise, if people knew how great Heaven was and how terrible Hell was, they could surely avoid Hell and go to Heaven.

The sun set, and darkness fell in the valley. The artillery unit continued to fire flares, lighting up the area like daytime, but nothing moved. The day had ended for the Vietcong.

All the squad members sat around the camp, pleased with themselves and their victory. Their main concern was how many kills they would count and how many weapons they would collect the next day, and they worried that a Vietcong soldier may have survived to strip the dead and run off with their weapons. It was common for enemy soldiers to carry off the guns and leave behind the corpses. Our squad leader suggested we go and check as early as possible the next morning because the number of guns plundered was more important to our side than the number of enemies killed.

2nd Squad (our squad) had wiped out the enemy, but we still had to stay up all night on emergency guard duty because we had given away our position. That night was pitch black and silent as death. As we listened attentively for any sound, we heard a moaning sound carried by the wind. It was hard to pinpoint where the sound came from. Someone said it must have been a dying enemy soldier.

The moon sailed in and out of dark clouds, and swarms of ravenous mosquitos tried to suck us dry before dawn came to chase them away. The other soldiers drank coffee from their canteens to stave off sleep. The night was long and tedious as we waited for morning.

Risking one's life

to kill

risking one's life

to live

The One in Heaven

the Creator of us all

speaks with rolls of thunder

like a thunderstorm

why are you trying to kill

the valuable lives

that I created?

They cannot hear
because their consciences are deaf

Love each other
then you will live.
Hatred, fighting
and war will end;
a world of peace
Heaven
and a world of love
will be fulfilled.

"LOVE HIM"

Dawn broke. Platoon leader J sent a message telling us to find out how many Vietcong had died and how many guns were left behind after the previous day's encounter. The squad leader told some soldiers to go and check, but they were all reluctant because checking the bodies carried a high risk of getting attacked by any of them that were left alive. Many soldiers had been shot dead while approaching what they thought was a corpse.

The Vietcong also put booby traps on corpses or weapons so that soldiers on our side would be killed when checking or moving them. Vietcong soldiers often carried valuables, including expensive watches, gold rings, gold necklaces, gold bracelets, and cash. So some people were hurt or even killed by their greed or recklessness while plundering enemy corpses. In this way, there were more than a few things to watch out for when undertaking the task of checking over the dead bodies on a battlefield.

Wearing a smile, the squad leader picked out me and Sergeant Yoo and sent us to go and check the corpses. We didn't want to go either, but we said we would. Looking down from the point where we had opened fire the previous day, we carefully scouted the area before heading into the valley. There were two very tall, beautiful trees next to some large rocks, so we made a mental note of the location and set off, carrying our radios.

We crept forward carefully through the rugged jungle and rocky terrain, moving just 5 meters, then checking for any sign of life, and then moving off again. We were extremely tense and were quickly bathed in sweat. After about an hour it seemed like we had reached our destination.

I could smell gunpowder too, so I felt we were almost there, but when we searched around, we couldn't see any corpses or any debris from the engagement. From above, it seemed like it would be easy to find the large trees and rocky areas we were aiming for, but once in the valley, we couldn't figure out where we were.

We contacted the rest of the squad using our radios and told them we couldn't find the right place. They asked where we were, but the jungle was so full of trees that we couldn't answer that either.

The squad leader told us we should follow the valley and should head back up, so we turned and headed uphill. From above, it seemed like we were only 100 meters off, but on the ground, it was difficult to find the right place, and we ended up travelling 200 meters through the large rocks to avoid the leafy jungle areas.

Sergeant Yoo was getting impatient, sweating like a pig and gulping down the water in his canteen. He took the lead and held his gun at his hip, the safety mechanism disengaged in case he saw an enemy and needed to use it. He crept forward, muscles tensed, carefully stepping across the mossy, slippery rocks. He motioned with his hands for me to come.

I climbed the slope about 6 meters behind him, equally anxious. Yoo looked back at me and pointed to indicate that we had almost reached the destination. A large rock, two meters high, was blocking our way, so Yoo climbed up over it, agile as a monkey.

I was waiting for him to give me a signal to climb up once he had checked what was ahead, but no signal came. I thought it must be safe, so I went and climbed up. There was a convenient rock I used to step up, and I held my gun in one hand and grabbed the rock with the other hand to climb.

But when I cleared the boulder, I was shocked to see Yoo sprawled out on his face, having dropped his gun on the rock and lost his helmet too.

I was stunned and stood there looking around frantically. Three meters in front of me, I saw a big tree with a wide trunk, about an arm span and a half in diameter, and half of a man's face sticking out behind it. He was pointing his gun directly at me.

Our eyes connected. He was eyeing me threateningly down the barrel of a gun, ready to shoot. All of a sudden, I went completely stiff. I felt dizzy, and my vision started to go black at the edges. I stared at him, eyes wide, as he pointed his gun at me, but I had no strength even to raise my own gun to my shoulder or aim it. Since he was hiding behind a large tree, I could only see half a face and one knee.

Yoo must have gone into shock on seeing the Vietcong soldier. I felt the same way, like I was barely conscious. As I stood there in a daze, stiff as a totem pole, he sharpened his aim while keeping his body side-on and protected by the tree. He was waiting for a response on purpose, because of what we had done to his unit the night before: I felt like he was just waiting to shoot, saying, "You guys are dead in my hands."

At that moment, I could not even manage a yell. I thought, 'This rock is where I will die. I lived through 22 years of hardships just to die here. How pointless my life was. On the battlefield, death comes in an instant. I had no idea this day would come!'

| A Vietcong was pointing his gun at me, hiding behind a tree. |

Then I heard a spiritual voice.

"How far will the boat go?"

"The boat can go only as far as the water reaches," I replied.

"How far will the train travel from Seoul?" The voice asked.

"It can go only as far as the end of the rail."

Right away I heard the voice in my heart: "So, too, the end of your life has come. It is over."

"Ah," I thought, "so I'm dying. I realized it a few seconds beforehand, and now I'm going to die."

My death was inevitable, and nothing could delay it even one more minute. I had no time to call my mother or father. I wanted to say my last prayers, but the gunshot would go off soon, and I wouldn't have even that much time.

Who could save me in that moment? Even if my dear parents knew what was happening, there was nothing they could do. Their love could not save me, nor could a king, no matter his power, nor could my fellow soldiers, who were too far away to help even if they had known what was going on.

The squad leader had sent us out to check the corpses left behind on the battlefield, but it seemed the whole squad became very lax and almost negligent. 'Who, in this whole world, can help me?' There was no hope of salvation except in the Almighty, Omnipotent and Omnipresent God. So I called on God and Jesus to save my life.

The Vietcong soldier saw me dazed and confused, and angled his body even further behind the tree, while aiming his gun squarely at my chest.

His eyes blazed with hatred, feeding my terror. And then I let go, I resigned myself to whatever fate heaven had for me, closed my eyes, and called God in my heart.

At that moment, I heard a voice from heaven.
It was loud and majestic.
"Love him!"
Only God's voice could sound like that: both frightening and lovely, shaking the mountains with such power that surely the whole world could hear it. No sound on earth is like it, and no human voice could come close. It shook me free from my stupor and I answered in my heart,
"If I love him, if I even move, won't I be killed?"

It seemed that if I made the slightest movement he would shoot me right away. Even though I was holding a gun, it was useless because I was out of my mind. I hesitated and stood there dumbly.

I heard the voice a second time.
"Love~~~~~~ him~~~~~~."
"If I go there, he'll kill me," I said, but there was no more reply.
I felt like death was mere moments away.
If I stayed still, I would be killed. If I moved, I would be killed too. So I decided to obey that voice from Heaven. That first step forward was as difficult as a thousand steps, but once I had lifted my heavy foot, strength came to my heart and body, and I was released from my rigid posture.

I took a second step, staring my enemy right in the eyes.
He stared back intently through his rifle scope, watching me approach.
I had heard a voice from heaven, and I said to myself, 'If I perish, I perish."

At that moment, the enemy looked like my sister.

In shock, I threw down my gun and ran forward.

"Youngja! What are you doing here?" I called my sister, hugged her and started to cry. I wept openly, and when I finally looked down, I realized I was embracing my enemy.

I was hugging the Vietcong soldier and crying. "Why do I have to kill you when you never hurt me? Why do you have to kill me when I've done nothing to you?" He hugged me back and wept loudly as if in agreement. By some miracle we could understand each other despite the language barrier.

If you think about it, neither he nor I had any reason to kill each other, but my country had sent me to the battlefield and my commanding officers had ordered me to kill the enemy. Since my enemy and I met under such circumstances, on opposite sides of the conflict, we ended up aiming guns at each other. Our leaders had assured us that killing the enemy was the only path to peace, and under that aim they sent us to fight on the battlefield, but of course, it was the powerless soldiers on the frontlines who paid with their lives.

Casting our guns aside, the soldier and I embraced and cried for maybe 40 minutes. After that, he seemed to remember something, and reached down to get something underneath him with a surprised expression. I asked what was going on, punctuating my words by shaking his shoulder, but he pushed my hand away and indicated that I should step back.

I guessed why he was slowing inching himself up off the ground and said I would take care of the dangerous task, reaching around under him but he shook his head determinedly. A little later, he pulled a grenade out that he had been sitting on and grasped it tightly. The grenade had no safety pin.

| ALL OF A SUDDEN, THE ENEMY LOOKED LIKE MY SISTER, SO I RAN TO HIM
CALLING MY SISTER'S NAME. |

| I THREW DOWN MY GUN, HUGGED THE ENEMY, AND WEPT. |

He had already unpinned the grenade and was sitting on it. I sensed that he wanted to throw it and was warning me to get down so that I didn't get hurt. This soldier had tried to shoot me just a short time earlier, but now he was telling me to be careful. That really touched me.

I told him, "You can't throw it that far because you're sitting down, so let me do it," and I tried to take the grenade from him. But without the pin, the grenade was too dangerous to pass to me, so he threw it 10 meters behind the large rock. After a pause, it exploded with a boom, shattering the silence of the mountains.

I discovered that the Vietcong soldier had been shot in the knee, and that's why he couldn't escape. He had been waiting for us to come and check the corpses, and had planned to kill himself and us with the grenade under his butt.

The grenade could easily have gone off in those 40 minutes while we had been sobbing in each other's arms – it was a miracle that it didn't. No one could explain why it hadn't exploded when I grabbed his arms and shook him, thinking he was my sister.

Even that soldier forgot he was sitting on a live grenade: that whole time we were crying and hugging, it didn't cross his mind. I couldn't help but realize that God had saved us through his grace and power. Even though I knew that was the truth, it was still hard to fully grasp what the invisible, almighty One had done.

When he threw the grenade, it exploded with a deafening 'bang!' that tore through the valley. The rest of the squad, still at the top of the valley, started yelling and asking what was going on. I don't know what they had been doing until then and why they hadn't paged us even once, but when the grenade went off, they were shouting and trying to find out what kind of accident had happened. I yelled back at them to come down and help us.

The explosion also woke Sergeant Yoo, who had passed out from shock when he had seen the enemy aiming a gun at him. He jumped up and was about to shoot both me and the Vietcong. Perhaps he had fallen asleep after passing out, but in any case, he was about to do something crazy after waking up suddenly like that. I yelled at him: "Hey! It's me, Jeong," but it was if he couldn't see me because of the enemy in front of him.

Yoo woke up with the memory of seeing his enemy down the barrel of a gun fresh in his mind, so his response was to shoot back. Those M16 guns held 21 bullets, and just touching the trigger set them off like a beehive exploding into chaos. Yoo wasn't even fully conscious of what he was doing but instinctively raised his gun to shoot us, so I quickly ran and grabbed it from him. Yoo yelled at me like I was crazy, asking why I didn't shoot the enemy.

I grabbed him around the neck and shouted back, furious: "Are you going to shoot me too?" I shook him until he came to his senses and realized that I wasn't the enemy, and as I kept talking, he calmed down and stopped being upset.

There were so many ways the situation could have ended in disaster. I was almost shot and killed by the Vietcong soldier. Then I was almost killed by the grenade he was sitting on. Then I was almost killed by Yoo who came back from unconsciousness without grasping what was going on. In that one place, I could have been killed three times, but I survived.

Even while writing this, I wondered: 'Did death avoid me, did I escape death, or did God Almighty save me?' Death doesn't avoid people, nor could I escape it: I can hear God in my conscience telling me that He saved me to use my life even until this day.

Yoo said that we should quickly tie up the Vietcong captive, but I retorted: "He saved us – why don't you trust him? Why do you want to tie him up?" He was just a young man, and his pale, slim face looked trusting and naïve. On seeing me speak up for him, he was so moved he teared up, and he willingly handed over his gun.

We decided to sit him down where there was a little flat space and question him until the rest of the squad showed up, but when I grabbed his hand to help him up, he couldn't stand. He screamed in pain, cradling his knee. I rolled up his pants leg to investigate and found he had been shot in the hamstring, with a bullet stuck halfway through his knee. That was when we realized why he had been sitting there waiting to kill us: he couldn't get away because he had been shot the night before.

I could tell the bullet was causing him terrible pain, so I wanted to remove it, but he pushed my hands away with a ghastly expression on his face. Even Yoo felt sorry on seeing him and said he needed a medic urgently. Then he shouted into the radio for our medic to hurry down to our location.

The other squad members above were in a bit of a panic and asked if we had been injured, so we explained that it wasn't us but one of the enemy soldiers who needed treatment. That made them laugh out loud. They had no idea what had happened.

BLOODLINE OF FAITH

We helped the Vietcong soldier move to somewhere flat, and the three of us sat facing each other. Our guns and cartridge belts had long been cast aside, and we sat peacefully. The Vietcong soldier pulled a gold necklace out from under his shirt, and I saw it was a cross, sparkling in the sun. I was shocked but also extremely moved.

At that moment, it occurred to me that he was Christian, just as I was. So I asked him, "Christian?" and he nodded. I told him that I was Christian, pulling out my pocket Bible and saying, "Bible, Bible." He was delighted too, grasping my hands joyfully: we belonged to the same family of faith. I embraced him again and wept.

He hugged me back. Truly, war is so cruel. War compels people from the same family of faith to even kill each other.

In the end, we are all brothers and sisters in God whether we believe in God or not. I realized that was why the Vietcong soldier had been shown to me as my sister. Yet, brothers and sisters were fighting and killing each other. This is why Jesus told us to love our enemies, to love God, and to love our brothers and sisters with our whole heart, soul and life.

God sees how a person acts in the face of death and whether he spares his enemy's life. God treats him as a brother if he treats his enemy as a brother. God treats him as His beloved if he treats his enemy with love. God makes miracles happen for those who love. Only fighting the battle of love can bring peace and bring about an end to the cruelty of war and conflict.

God made me realize about the path of peace and love for mankind, a path without cursing and hatred and wars. So it was impossible for me to shoot my enemy – to kill my brothers. Instead, I turned my gun around and pointed it at the sky, risking my own life to save my enemy even when it was impossible to capture him.

It is right and proper for people to live by their own conscience and skills. Gradually, nations began to realize this for themselves, and they were able to cast aside their weapons of war and treat each other as brothers. A new era of love and peace dawned across the world as that cursed war gradually came to an end.

The cross necklace the Vietcong soldier wore was three times bigger than the crosses most Christians wore. I guess he was Catholic, and he told me yes, he was. Catholics and Protestants are also brothers and sisters of the same faith. He removed his necklace and watch and gave them to me, but I said I didn't need them and put the necklace back on him. He removed it again and said that the spoils of war go to the victor. I usually would not have been able to understand that much Vietnamese, but somehow we could freely communicate on that day. That was God's miracle, too.

I told him that it was not a matter of victors and losers, but that we had both won because we didn't die and didn't shoot each other. He gave me the watch and necklace again, so I let him put the necklace on me. I could see Yoo looking covetously at the watch, so I fastened it on Yoo's wrist. Yoo tried to pretend he didn't want it at first, but then was happy to receive it and couldn't help asking if it was a Swiss brand.

Back then, Koreans really loved foreign brands, including anything made in America. They still love foreign luxury items, so you can imagine how highly such things were valued 45 years ago when they were almost unobtainable. Yoo couldn't read English, so he asked me whether the watch was American or Swiss, but I couldn't read it either. I couldn't ask the Vietcong soldier about it, but from its appearance, it looked like a Swiss design.

So I told Yoo the watch was made in Switzerland and that it was very expensive. He was very pleased with it, and hid it under his sleeve, asking me not to tell the squad leader about it.

Normally, Vietcong soldiers carried long-barreled, single shot rifles, but this Vietcong had an assault rifle which could shoot many times in a row. I explained to him that I had heard God's tremendous voice commanding me to love him, and that's why I had run and hugged him. He said that he had also felt somehow moved to respond at that moment.

I asked how many other soldiers had been with him yesterday, and he said there had been many, but they had moved to another location. His platoon had also been on the move when they were attacked. When he pointed us in the right direction, we saw many corpses and weapons scattered through the jungle.

That really brought us to our senses. Looking at all those corpses made our hearts pound and our hair stand on end: what if other soldiers had been shot but not killed, and were hiding behind the rocks? Yoo and I climbed to a higher rock so that we could look around carefully. We saw more bodies lying on the other side of the slope, and all the big trees and rocks that the Vietcong had tried to shelter behind were riddled with bullet marks from the intense assault.

The medic and the rest of our platoon got lost while trying to find us, so they were very sweaty and out of breath when they finally arrived. I showed the medic where the Vietcong soldier had been shot in the knee, and he said that removing the bullet would cause heavy bleeding, so he should be evacuated instead. Then we began the task of checking dead bodies and collecting weapons.

We were only able to check the bodies on the lower side of the slope, since there was a risk of being exposed to surviving Vietcong snipers on the upper side. Yoo and I asked the other squad members to go one more time and search for bodies, but they were afraid, and they just looked around quickly and said there weren't any more. We identified nine corpses that day, and collected eight guns, including the one from the surviving Vietcong soldier.

After finishing the operation, I carried the Vietcong down the mountain on my back. The rest of the squad made their way 100 meters to the foot of the mountain, struggling to carry our spoils. After everyone had come down the mountain, the whole platoon gathered.

A MINOR SKIRMISH WITH A VIETCONG SOLDIER HIDING IN A CAVE

Platoon Leader J was pleased to see the soldier we had taken captive and the weapons, and congratulated our platoon. He ordered the rest of the squad to leave their packs behind and carefully search all the nearby caves, since we could not let our guard down without making a thorough search of the area.

Each squad split up for the search as instructed. Our squad located one cave and saw signs that someone was there. On checking, we determined that an enemy soldier was inside.

We promised the Vietcong soldier that if he laid his gun on the ground and came out with his hands up, he would not be killed, but he was afraid and didn't come out. We shone our flashlights near the entrance of the cave and shouted at him to hurry up and surrender. He fired at us in response, so we were forced to change our strategy.

He was like a rat in a trap, and would easily have been killed if we just threw a grenade in the cave, but we wanted to capture him alive. We spent an hour sweating in the heat and risking our lives as we continued to try to take him prisoner.

That natural cave was only 10 meters long and not very wide. Using our flashlights, we could see the soldier lying flat on the ground. He didn't seem to be moving anywhere, so we fired shots at the cave ceiling and walls. We didn't shoot the soldier, but the cave filled up with the smell of gunpowder and dust from the pulverized rocks.

After nothing else happened for a while, we investigated again and found him stretched out on the ground, not moving. He seemed dead, so we felt it was safe to go inside, but he had actually fallen down and passed out. When we dragged him out into the sunlight, he didn't have any bullet wounds or other injuries, and he regained consciousness after about half an hour.

One after another, the soldiers in my squad shouted at him and tapped his head. "You idiot, it wouldn't have been so bad if you'd just come out the first time we told you." He was malnourished and looked like he had suffered greatly. He was brought before the platoon leader, who stared at him in his usual manner and said, "Look at this skinny bitch. A puny guy like you doesn't stand a chance against us!"

The squad leader shouted at him so much even the mountains would have felt embarrassed. When he shouted, "Giơ tay lên!" which means, "Hands up!" the Vietcong was surprised and raised his hands. The squad leader kept asking, "Where are the others who were with you?" But he didn't reply. After shouting at him to "Tôi sẽ giết bạn!" which means "I'll kill you!" he understood and changed his mind about speaking to us.

He said that he and his comrades had been moving all around the mountain the previous night, and he was the only one left behind to keep watch on the enemy. He referred to the group we had fired on at sunset, and we asked him where their guns had been hidden. He pointed us in that direction, so we immediately took him with us to search for the guns.

We found a stash of personal firearms covered with grease and wrapped in paper so that they would not be damaged by rust if they stayed there for some time. The discovery of those firearms was considered a major success, following on from the previous day's successes.

"UNCONSCIONABLE"

With the search operation complete, it was time for lunch. Each squad set up their tent and ate. While we were eating, a big explosion suddenly went off nearby. In shock, we knocked over our ration tins and got down on the ground, while clay and stone debris rained around us. Everyone was yelling and asking what happened, but a voice out the front said to calm down because everything was ok.

We could see bits of bloody flesh staining the tent we had erected, and the stink of blood filled the air. The smell was so bad that it was impossible to eat anything else. After the explosion, bits of flesh had fallen from the air with the dirt and rocks.

We made a call on the squad radio, and found out that one of the officers had taken the Vietcong soldier Yoo and I had found in the valley that morning. He had tried to extract information from him, but when the Vietcong hadn't given him anything, he had murdered him with a Claymore mine.

That officer was the scariest man in the entire unit. Even during our training phase, he had disciplined his subordinates so strictly that they all behaved like cats in front of a tiger. He intimidated them so much that they said even his shadow made their hair stand on end. As for me, a naïve kid from the countryside, I was even more scared of his voice and his discipline. Should I compare him to a burning hot pepper, or the hardness of steel, or a wild hyena? Even his smile was terrifying, and we were afraid even when he was in a good mood.

Despite all that, when I heard that he had killed the captive Vietcong, I was furious. I went straight up to him and demanded to know why he had killed the enemy I had captured, who had never even tried to hurt him. The officer had made him stand in front of a Claymore mine and blown it up with a detonator, tearing his body to pieces, and now he was sitting calmly in his tent.

I asked him how he could brutally murder the enemy soldier who had spared Yoo and myself. He answered that the enemy hadn't answered any questions, so he had killed him. I snapped at him, "Isn't it proper to be thankful that he saved your subordinates, and spare him? Are you so callous?" And I told him that God was angry, seeing what he had done.

"Even an enemy becomes an ally if he surrenders and comes over to our side, so isn't it right to love him? If we take the enemy's weapons, we don't destroy them because they belong to us now. Isn't it by the same logic that we shouldn't kill a soldier who is now on our side?" I pierced his conscience with those words. In fact, it was God speaking through my lips.

The officer listened to me and seemed convicted of his cruelty. "You would have saved him, but I could not. I couldn't control my anger and I used the Claymore mine to tear his body to pieces." I replied, fuming, that even though the Vietcong were our enemies, cruelty to them would rebound back on our side. I told him that the captive soldier was a believer, and asked him what God and Jesus would think about what he had done.

"A life is repaid with a life, so if you want to live, you had better save others. Those who don't want to die should save their enemies, then God will protect both the Commander and his subordinates. This is not my word, but Heaven's word." I told him boldly.

Neither God nor I could hold back our rebuke, since he had killed the man I had captured at the risk of my own life. Those who didn't realize as I had realized just kept hating others and tried to solve their problems with guns.

After hearing me out, he laughed at me. "I don't believe in Jesus, so how can I do such a thing? If you become the Commander, you try living like that." I told him that I wasn't the only one unable to eat lunch because of the stench of blood he had inflicted on the whole unit, and that he should have spared the Vietcong soldier. He replied that if we went hungry for long enough, we wouldn't have any trouble keeping our food down. He absolutely refused to understand what I was trying to say, so I gave up and went back to my squad.

I told the others what he had done, and they all agreed that he should have saved the enemy. Behind his back, they all said he had cruelly killed the soldier, and called him evil and spiteful. They told each other in undertones that there was no reason to inflict such brutality on the enemy. The squad's collective opinion of his deeds was in sync with God's view.

God watches with eyes like flames to see how a man will choose between good and evil. I could feel God's intense fury on that day. I wondered, 'Why did he cruelly murder a soldier who had been taken captive? He should not have done that. God will repay him according to his deeds.'

I felt a weight of sin on my own shoulders, since I had failed to protect my Vietcong friend in the end. I felt so sorry for him. When I had brought him down the mountain, he had thanked me for not shooting him, and I had told him not to be afraid, since I wouldn't let anyone kill him. I had no idea that my superior officer would do such a terrible thing.

I thought, 'He would still be alive if I had stayed with him.' Sadly, I entrusted his spirit to the Lord. I told him to be my friend in spirit, since we would no longer meet in body. Although his body was destroyed, my friend's spirit rests comfortably in the arms of God.

That incident shook me to the core. I valued my enemy's life and captured him, yet he had still been killed. The weight of grief in my heart made me think perhaps it was better to let the enemies escape than to try to catch them. God made me think of the enemy as my own family by showing my sister's face in place of his. God enlightened me that killing an enemy is as evil as killing a brother. Even on the battlefield, there is a time to kill and a time to save: to kill the one you should save is truly wicked.

Meditation in the Jungle

My life
when I am struggling alone
with life on the battlefield
Somewhere I hear a voice
'Love lives.
I created mankind.'

Surely that spiritual voice,
sounding not in my ears but in my heart,
is the voice of God
who created all mankind

Oh, how we live
in opposition to His purpose
I turn my eyes away
from the tragic world
looking up at the sky.
The God of Heaven, the Creator

is watching

all mankind

to see how they are living today

In shame

I cannot lift my head

to look at the sky

I open my eyes

and stare at the ground

I am so distressed

to see my brothers on the earth.

I weep secret tears

they fall to the ground

one drop, two drops, three drops.

I heard the rest of the story later, after I was discharged. I heard from some other Vietnam veterans that the regimental commander had heard about the POW I captured being killed and had praised the senior officer for his boldness. He was promoted and put in charge of an APC (Armored Personnel Carrier) and ended up stuck in the most dangerous theater of the war for six months. That was a place like hell, full of the horrors of death and brutal hardships. It reminded me of what it says in the Bible, that people are repaid for their deeds, whether through blessings or suffering.

I was reminded of that senior officer in 1998 and sent some people to find out what had happened to him. They found that he had passed away a few years earlier in a gas poisoning accident. Sadly, he didn't live beyond his 40s. His fate reminded me once again of the way he had used the Claymore mine to kill the Vietcong soldier who saved me and whom I captured after that battle on Chai Mountain.

I still remember rebuking him as God inspired me: that even an enemy should not be killed cruelly like that, and that it is wrong to act with evil or cruelty, whether on the battlefield or in life.

Life Guarantee 1

When you meet the enemy,
whoever shoots first
can live

Love your enemy
Love your neighbor as yourself
Jesus' Words
come to my heart

I should love my enemy
in order for me to live.

I think about this
but there is no guarantee
that the enemy will not shoot
just because I
do not shoot him

But I first
put down my gun
my faith is only
in God Almighty
who saves me.
I must
obey His Word.

Ah!
The enemy lives
I live

I'm still alive because
We both live.
Even today I testify for the One
and I love Him.

In the battle
I performed a miracle
of not shooting the enemy
who was about to shoot me
God also performed a miracle
so that the enemy
would not
shoot me.

Life Guarantee 2

The last day
of my life
a gun was pointed
at my chest

I entrusted my life
to Heaven
and waited, eyes closed
for Him to act

The mountains rang
the fields rang
with His voice
from the sky

"Love Him"
"Love Him"
Obeying that word
my enemy and I
both lived

Later I found
that he and I
were brothers in God
we embraced each other
moved to tears

By loving each other,
we became friends
we became brothers.
Everyone on this earth
is my brother, my sister.

Brothers fight and kill
Because of different ideologies,
different mentalities
That is war.
If you love each other, it is heaven
If you hate each other, it is hell.
Love brings life;
Hatred brings death.

The enemy saved me
My superior should have cared
Should have praised him and treated him well
My enemy, who believed in the same God
Who waited, helpless like a sheep
Hoping to survive

How could any man with a conscience
Brutally blow him to pieces?
I still recall
The stench of his blood

Those who witnessed his deed
Condemned it
His brutality
His vicious cruelty

Tears fell, my heart ached
I cried out to heaven
for the death of the soldier
who saved me

Heaven's fury
burst forth
"His deeds will be repaid"
I heard in my heart

Though he lived 40 years

He is no more

Though I call

He cannot answer

Only the nightingale remains

Crying sadly

Even these days, you may have heard in the news about POWs being captured and brutally treated or killed in war zones. The whole world would agree that such cruelty is unwarranted. To kill the Vietcong soldiers after they turned away from the past and cooperated with our allies, seeking freedom, was unspeakably cruel.

Let me tell you what happened to the other Vietcong POW – the one our squad found in the cave. We didn't kill him but fed him C-ration for lunch to fill his empty stomach. Later, we took him away in the same helicopter that carried the arms we found and confiscated based on his information.

As for us, that operation was followed by another week-long ambush mission on Chai Mountain. Sixteen enemy soldiers approached our ambush and would have been killed, but I managed to warn them of our presence and they fled, alive. I still carried the guilt of failing to protect the Vietcong prisoner I captured on that mountain: I promised he wouldn't die, but my superior officer killed him, so I felt guilty before both God and the Vietcong.

THE BAD HABIT OF DRINKING

When I think about that officer, his drinking habit also comes to mind. At the time, he was close to me. He trusted me because of my lifestyle: I didn't drink and basically lived an ascetic life of faith. He would sometimes walk into the squad barracks, and if he saw me reading the Bible, he would smile and greet me saying, "Chaplain, how are you?" although he didn't have faith himself.

In several conversations with him, I told him how important it was for especially leaders to believe in God and pray, so that the men under them would be protected from the dangers of the battlefield and their military operations would be successful. His response was, "I don't need to believe in God because you believe in Him. I look after you so that you can live a life of faith, but for me, I'm not going to believe in Jesus because I don't want to have to repent every day for drinking."

People who don't live a life of faith all have excuses. They say they don't want to attend church because they don't like the pastor, or because there is in-fighting at church, or because they would have to give money to the church. My superior officer asked me to repent for him, and said he would look after me in exchange, and he did, in fact, treat me better than anyone else for that reason. God made him love me since I love God.

Once, at a unit party, he tried everything to make me drink. When I kept refusing, he was so upset he poured a glass of alcohol over my head. He said he was giving me a direct order, and then, since he would lose face in front of his subordinates if I continued to refuse, he begged me to at least pretend to drink. So I took one sip of the wine, and then I spat it out.

Then he boasted that he had broken my record of never drinking. Lowering his voice to an offensive whisper, he even said he would take me the next time he went to sleep with girls, too. The other soldiers, who were drunk, shouted their approval, saying, "Let's all go out this week." When senior officers or seniors in the workplace try to force those under them to drink, it shows a complete lack of manners and lack of respect for others.

After that, everyone went to spend their time off in the village, and that senior officer sent me a message through the dispatch officer: "Let's go to town to meet girls and have fun." I replied, "Please don't even say something like that, because I'm never going there – I'm not even going to think about going there." Even the dispatch officer felt sorry for being involved, and told me he knew I wouldn't go but had no choice but to relay the officer's message.

People's minds work in such a way that they always want other people to join in what they're doing, without even thinking about whether what they're doing is right or wrong. Then they get angry or petulant with those who don't want to join in, and even make nasty comments or spread rumors about them. They do that because they're ignorant. I couldn't say anything to my superior officer, but in my mind I said, 'Even if I'm the only one, I must do what is righteous so that you and all these soldiers won't be killed before your time. When will you grow up and realize about me?'

Most of the time, though, he joked around and was friendly and helpful to me because I would act as his dispatch rider, even though he already had one.

Early in 1967, our company was stationed near the village of Furong at the foot of Honba Mountain. One time, I told him about the atmosphere in our squad and said that Sergeant H hated me for no reason, and whenever he drank, he would take the end pieces out of his bed and beat me or some other squad member. When my superior officer heard that, he was furious. He said, "That bastard. Does he want to die? You guys are not his subordinates but my subordinates." Then he ordered the fugleman to bring him in.

The reality was that Sergeant H drank alcohol like it was water or any other drink. He didn't drink so much when we were on a search operation, but he still carried beer in his pack and drank from time to time. He was addicted to alcohol and drank even on the battlefield, and when he drank, he went crazy and took out his anger on the squad members. No one could control his drinking habit.

On the occasions when I managed to communicate with him, I tried to tell him not to drink so much – not because I didn't like the drinking but because of the way he harassed and mistreated the members of our squad whenever he drank. I warned him seriously that his health would fail and he would die young if he didn't control his drinking, but he was hardly going to stop because it had become his habit.

When Sergeant H was dragged in by the fugleman, he had been drinking again, and he smelt of alcohol. The officer told the fugleman to bring in the end pieces of the bed, and he hit the fugleman across the back several times to demonstrate. Then he told the fugleman, "Beat Sergeant H like I showed you, but just don't kill him."

The fugleman was angry after being beaten. He made Sergeant H hold a push-up position and hit him without mercy. "It's your job to look after

your subordinates, not to harass and beat them. You deserve this beating."
He said. Sergeant H was sprawled out on the concrete floor of the unit
headquarters like a limp frog.

I watched that beating thinking that it was God's judgement. At the same
time, though, I worried that he would treat us even worse after the beating.
I told the fugleman to stop. The officer spoke to Sergeant H. "You're a
drunk, you disrespected my position, and you just did whatever you wanted.
I was going to thrash you within an inch of your life when the chance came,
and today was that day."

Even the officer had felt bad about the Sergeant drinking so much and
causing trouble, but the officer hadn't yet had sufficient justification to
have him beaten. That day provided the perfect opportunity to punish
him for tormenting the squad members. The officer told us to report to
him immediately if Sergeant H got drunk and hit us again.

Still, that drunken sot was beyond reformation. Less than a month later,
he was back to harassing us to an intolerable degree. We couldn't go back
and tell the officer because we would end up in an even worse position
afterwards. What we ended up doing was putting on all our gear and
leaving the base to get as far away from him as possible. When the
company commander found out what we had done, Sergeant H would be
held responsible, and we wanted him to get into trouble.

We called up Company Commander Min on the two-way radio at 1 a.m.
that night. He answered and asked who was speaking, so we explained
that we were 1st Platoon, 2nd Squad, and we had left the company base.

Someone chimed in that it would be easier to live with the enemy because of 'someone' who drank too much and beat us.

Commander Min said he would take responsibility for the situation and told us to return to base. We replied that it wasn't the responsibility of the platoon leader or the company commander. We explained that his drinking was so bad there were rumors about it through the entire company and that his conduct would be unbecoming even by a civilian. But even so, he hadn't been disciplined. Company Commander Min coaxed us to return, not to the platoon, but to his office to discuss the matter further.

We eventually decided to go and talk to him. When we entered his office, he asked what was going on, "You're good men, so tell me what's wrong. What's on your mind?" We repeated what we'd told him over the radio and asked him to deal with the drunken Sergeant who was beating us. He promised to take care of it and spoke to the superior officer who already knew the situation, so we went there and explained ourselves over again.

The officer asked why we hadn't reported the problem to him and berated us for leaving the base instead. He ordered Sergeant H to be brought in immediately. H had been drinking again and had fallen asleep without knowing that anything was going on.

Sergeant H reeked of alcohol. The officer hit him in the knee. "You bastard, is this a battlefield or your bedroom?" Suddenly alert, H asked, "Why are you doing this?" The officer screamed in his face, "Do you want me to beat you to death?" He beat H like a dog with the end pieces of the bed and shouted himself hoarse, "You bastard, you should've been afraid of me."

However, even the officer didn't think he'd be able to refrain from drinking without further inducement. He made him sign a note saying that his punishment for drinking any more than one drink in a day would be a severe beating. The law was laid down for him on that day. Sergeant H scowled that he would rather not drink at all under those conditions. The officer laughed in his face and said, "Hey bitch, can a mutt hold back when it wants to eat shit?" He knew H was an alcoholic and that it would be impossible to stop him from drinking.

Sergeant H took us back to our squad post mumbling promises to change interspersed with accusations that we'd ratted on him. He was too afraid to hit us, but he still took his anger out on us in other ways by not letting us sleep. We were helpless to do anything because that's what the army is like. We couldn't kill him or get back at him. He was more hateful than the enemy. He didn't change his drinking habits even after being punished by the higher-ups.

While I was writing this book, I contacted an old friend, Park Jung-bae, to ask him some questions about our time in Vietnam. He was one of my squad members and came from a place called Jinhae by the sea. I served with him in the same company and platoon on both my tours of Vietnam.

We were friends in Vietnam, and after returning to Korea, we met once or twice a year and often spoke on the phone. He was an AR (automatic rifle) shooter in our squad. Although he had a passionate side, he generally managed to keep his cool and ended up taking care of the squad better than the squad leader did, often taking on the more difficult jobs. He was neat and clean. He looked out for the other squad members when we were on operation or when they needed help with something.

So I got in touch with him again, 30 years after our time in Vietnam, and asked if he remembered anything about Sergeant H. He only remembered that Sergeant H drank a lot and used to beat us. He said, "I don't even want to think about how many beatings we took back then."

Alcohol is harmful to society and to families as well as in the military. People don't realize just how much their drinking hurts the people around them. Many people die or face other kinds of ruin because of alcohol.

During the war, there was a view that alcohol gave the men courage to fight more boldly, so nothing was done to stop soldiers from drinking. Sergeant H would have agreed that drinking himself into a rage and beating his subordinates made him feel better. Although more than 45 years have passed, it still makes me angry to think about it, so I've recorded his story in history.

ONLY WHEN THINGS ARE DONE GOD'S WAY CAN EVERYONE LIVE

God is truly alive. Just as I shared with you, I heard His voice in that epic life-or-death moment on Chai Mountain when the Vietcong soldier was about to shoot me. Without that voice, I would have died because I didn't know what to do. I was able to live through loving my enemy. I was able to live by obeying God's word. I had reached the limits of my own ability to keep myself alive.

Through that incident, I confirmed my belief that God alone could save me, and there was no future in living by my own will. If I'd done things my own way, the enemy and I both would both have died. By doing things God's way, we both lived. In that situation where we should have been killed, we survived by obeying God's word, which was to 'love your enemy.'

Even today, I teach those who follow me to live the same way. Whenever I am faced with extreme difficulties, I remember that story and I hear God's voice in my heart, "Love him. You must love him; then you and he will both live." Although it is difficult and sometimes very painful, I put my life on the line to obey those words and to live.

There is a level of grace that God grants to every person in the world. The rain falls and the sun shines on the wicked as well as the righteous. However, we must realize that people are all repaid according to their deeds, their hearts, and how they treat God, other people, and even nature.

Each person must realize that God saved them at that moment of death just as He saved me, no matter that the situation was different to mine. Know this, and respond to God with thanksgiving and love from this point onward. Then the infinite blessings of God will fill both your body and spirit.

In the same way, only the battle of love, fought in the way God wants, can end the warring, hatred, and fighting between individuals and even nations.

Made in the USA
Middletown, DE
06 May 2022